ERNST SARTORIUS

The Doctrine of the Person and Work of Christ

JUST SINNER
PUBLISHING HOUSE

First published by Just and Sinner 2020

First edition

ISBN: 978-1-952295-23-2

This book was professionally typeset on Reedsy.
Find out more at reedsy.com

Contents

INTRODUCTION

Ernst Wilhelm Christian Sartorius (1797-1859), was a German orthodox Lutheran theologian with a prolific theological career. Born at the zenith of the Enlightenment, he began his education when Friedrich Schleiermacher's rationalism was the most prevalent doctrinal approach in the European theological academy. Sartorius studied at Göttingen University and eventually became a professor at Tartu University.

Sartorius' career was characterized by his opposition to rationalism and his profound devotion to Christ. Unlike many of his theological contemporaries, Sartorius was strictly orthodox, holding to a high view of the inspiration of Scripture as well as traditional Constantinopolitan Christology. His work synthesizes sixteenth- and seventeenth-century Lutheran orthodoxy with a strong Augustinian piety.

The Doctrine of the Person and Work of Christ was put together from manuscripts of Sartorius' lectures on Christology given at Tartu University in 1831. These lectures discuss Christology and the work of Christ in the economy of salvation, treating numerous other aspects of Christian theology in a more incidental manner throughout. Sartorius' manner of proceeding is devotional rather than dogmatic, though traditional Lutheran systematic theology clearly undergirds his thought.

Like any theologian, Sartorius was not without his flaws. While living in Prussia he supported the Prussian Union of the Reformed and Lutheran churches, believing that the union church would take a generally Lutheran direction; sadly, the opposite result came about. He was also sympathetic to the controversial kenotic Christology of Thomasius, who posited a communication of attributes from Christ's human nature to His divinity, thus limiting the omniscience and power of Christ during His humiliation. Sartorius' sympathies toward this mode of thinking are apparent throughout these lectures. Despite these controversial aspects of Sartorius' thought, however, his work remains distinctly Lutheran, while at the same time bringing a salutary devotional fervor to doctrines which are often treated in a more scholastic manner.

1

GOD MANIFEST IN THE FLESH

THE SCRIPTURE DISCOVERIES OF "GOD MANIFEST IN THE FLESH," SHOWN TO BE MORE GLORIOUS THAN THE WONDERS OF ASTRONOMY.

THE lectures delivered in this place last year by Professor Struve on Popular Astronomy have induced me to undertake the present course with a similar design. Many of you listened with the deepest interest to those instructive and delightful discourses, which laid open to your view the vault of heaven and its precious treasures. I venture to hope that the contemplation of the spiritual heavens will not excite less, but rather greater, attention than that of the physical, since it has a closer relation to our hearts and lives. It is an object to which the attention has been directed at an earlier period of life, and which presents a greater variety of points that come into contact with the wants of our nature. Nor are these two departments of knowledge so very distant from one another, but in fact unite in leading us upwards to the same infinite being Whose character they combine to illustrate. That great truth which our eloquent instructor presented to you as the final result of His investigations—namely, that astronomy places in the most glorious light the omnipotence and wisdom of the Creator—is announced by the Holy Scriptures in the words of the Psalmist: "The heavens declare the glory of God; and the firmament showeth His handy work" (Ps. 19:1). They do indeed tell us great things of God and afford a bright display of His glory. Hence the psalmist in another passage exclaims with rapture, "O Lord my God, Thou art very great; Thou art clothed with honour and majesty; Who coverest Thyself with light as with a garment; Who stretchest out the heavens like a curtain" (Ps. 104:1). A mighty, overpowering discourse is addressed to us by the starry heavens, declaring in a splendid and glorious manner the majesty of God. The profoundest awe must pervade our spirits when we lift up our eyes to heaven and gaze on that garment of the Almighty, studded from the zenith to the horizon with ten thousand stars, which are not mere superficial ornaments, but immense worlds, glowing suns scattered by the Almighty through the regions of space, grouped into constellations as the decorations of His vesture, and, in the Milky Way, thickly interwoven as a splendid zone. The most ordinary mind must view with wonder the brilliancy of these Divine gems, sparkling with the purest luster, each one in magnitude a world and in splendor inferior only to the sun. But our admiration of the might and glory of the Most High rises still higher when the astronomer, having investigated the laws and plans of the Eternal Mind, unfolds and scientifically describes the wonderful arrangements by which these immense spheres upheld by the finger of God remain fixed in space with no movement but that of silently revolving on their axes; or, projected as a ball by the Divine hand, roll on with astonishing velocity, yet always keeping obediently their prescribed path, and, without losing any of those subordinate bodies which accompany them in their course through the light ether, arrive sooner or later, but always at the right time, to the very hour—yea, minute and second!—at the destined point in their orbits. We admire a good time-piece made by a skillful artist, but what a paltry piece of workmanship with its wheels, springs, and screws must this be compared with the celestial time-piece of our solar system, in which, without any mechanical adjustments, merely by the operations of an attractive and repulsive power, the planets revolve along with their satellites, and century after century with undeviating punctuality mark years and days, weeks and months, without needing any repair. And probably this solar system itself is but a mere watch compared with the great time-piece of the universe, in which our sun as a planet and the planets as its satellites move in strict order round a common center, while they cherish in their bosom the innumerable living beings entrusted to their care and obediently execute all the commands of their Lord.

Thus it is evident that the science of the stars leads directly to the acknowledgment of the most high God, and we find that in Holy Writ many of the sublimest illustrations of the Divine power and majesty are derived from this source. "Lift up your eyes on high, and behold Who hath created these things, that bringeth out their host by number: He calleth them all by names by the greatness of His might, for that He is strong in power; not one faileth" (Isa. 40:26). It is therefore a groundless assertion of mere sciolists that the extraordinary advances of astronomy in our times have given conceptions of God and of His relation to man at variance with the declarations of Scripture. I maintain on the contrary that they have only served to illustrate and confirm in a most glorious manner the scriptural character of God: for in proportion as they tend to give us more vivid impressions of the Divine greatness and omnipotence, they are conformable to the representations of the inspired writings. How forcibly is the littleness and insignificance of our earth contrasted with the greatness and infinitude of God, when it is described as being "the footstool of His throne!" "Behold," says the prophet Isaiah, "the nations are as a drop of a bucket, and are counted as the small dust of the balance; behold, He taketh up the isles, as a very little thing." The same prophet, in order to assist us in forming some notion of the Divine power, declares of Jehovah that He has "meted out heaven with a span" (Isa. 40:12); the countless millions of miles which separate us from those heavenly bodies are to the Almighty but as a span's length.

In fact, the discoveries made by modern science of the wonders of the Divine power must prove the folly of the assertion that the miracles recorded in the Bible are impossible. The opinions hastily formed by the multitude—who judge of things by superficial appearances and the experience of their senses, and reject whatever is not in accordance with these as inconceivable and impossible—are shown by the Copernican system to be completely fallacious and contemptible. Nothing appears more agreeable to experience and the order of nature than that the earth, with all the bodies and substances on its surface, stands still, and that the sun and stars are in motion. The language of common life is formed on such a conception, yet we know that the contrary is the fact: the earth, we all admit, revolves on its own axis, traveling round the sun with an amazing and yet (to us) imperceptible velocity. We are constantly pursuing our course through the boundless fields of space without leaving any traces of our progress. Owing to the immense distance of the fixed stars, the earth completes its annual revolutions without any apparent difference to us in their position; yet, however little indicated by appearances, this great movement takes place with undeviating regularity. If this be not wonderful, what is so? What fact in the Bible, physically considered, is so wonderful? The Ascension of Christ, Who by the Divine power, was borne beyond the narrow limits of this earth and rose to a higher region, considered as a mere physical event was a small matter compared with the suspension of the stars in empty space or with the conveyance of the planets and comets by the simple force of attraction through their immense orbits. What can be impossible to that Being Who performs such mighty works, Who with the rapidity of lightning, in the twinkling of an eye, forms into an harmonious system bodies so remote and without material contact causes them to operate energetically on one another, so that even our small moon powerfully affects the waters of the ocean? In truth, the miracles of the Bible, as one of the ancient fathers remarks, are not greater, but only more uncommon than those of nature. The parting of the Red Sea for the passage of the children of Israel was not a greater but only a more unusual occurrence than the daily ebb and flow of the immense ocean. The feeding of five thousand men with two barley loaves and a few small fishes was only a more unusual and rapid effecting of that which takes place every year on a much larger scale, by means of which the whole human race are provided with sustenance from a comparatively small quantity of grain. And that Being Who year after year can form the juice of the grape from the moisture of the ground and the action of the air on the sap-vessels of the vine can with equal ease change water into wine, as was actually performed at the marriage feast of Cana.

Thus the magnificent exhibition of the starry skies and indeed the whole sublime book of nature lead us to the knowledge of the same God of power and majesty, Whom the Bible in so plain and simple a manner reveals to our reason and conscience: "For the invisible things of Him from the creation of the world are clearly seen, being understood by the things that are made, even His eternal power and Godhead" (Rom. 1:20). But it may be asked: if reason and nature teach us so much, what need is there of a written revelation? In answer to this question much might be said on the use and advantage, and even the necessity, of a supernatural and written revelation in relation to natural religion, points which are fully discussed in schools of theology. I would, however, adduce on this occasion only the most weighty argument, which is at the same time adapted to set in a clear and striking point of view the mutual relation of theology and astronomy. The starry heavens reveal the infinite greatness and majesty of God to a vast, or rather an immeasurable, extent, surpassing our utmost conceptions. These myriads of worlds in infinite space, this host of stars and double stars of all magnitudes, this flood of suns poured along the Milky Way—our spirit turns giddy in breathless wonder and is oppressed to utter exhaustion by such transcendent vastness and magnificence. "Eagle-thought!" says Schiller in his lines on the greatness of the universe:

Eagle thought,
Let fall thy pinions:
Fancy, bold adventurous sailor,
Drop thine anchor in despair.

But the same poet in another passage confesses that there is something still more sublime than the material universe, for, addressing the astronomers, he says:

Your theme is indeed the most exalted in space;
But, my friends, the Sublime dwells not in space;

The Holy Scriptures present us with views of the Deity more exalted, more suited to excite our astonishment than that immeasurable and boundless grandeur of which we have been speaking—not by enlarging our views in that direction, but rather by narrowing and contracting them. However paradoxical this may appear, it is nevertheless true. It is glorious to be great and unlimited; it is sublime to be exalted and majestic; but it is grander and more sublime for greatness to humble itself, voluntarily to lay aside the splendor of majesty, and, out of love to the little and the low, to become little and low. It is great to wear a crown and wield a scepter, but it is greater voluntarily to renounce them. It is noble to ascend a throne and exercise dominion over others, but it is more noble to descend from a throne and, out of love, to become the servant of others. God is the Supreme Majesty—the King of kings, infinitely exalted eternal, almighty, illimitable. "The heaven of heavens cannot contain Him" (1 Kgs. 8:27). The revelations of Holy Scripture and the discoveries of astronomy unite in calling upon us to acknowledge Him as the Lord of glory. But the Scriptures exhibit to us what is indeed their principal object: along with that greatness of God in the great, His greatness also in the little; along with a greatness in height, a greatness in depth. Here we behold condescension in alliance with sublimity, compassion with omnipotence; the beams of Divine Majesty along with the veil that conceals their effulgence; the form of God and the form of a servant; and by this wonderful union and juxtaposition of attributes so opposite, we receive a far more powerful impression of each. For, naturally, the higher the station any one occupies, so much the more striking is his condescension; the greater his might and glory, so much the more remarkable is his humiliation. Since God is the Most High, He can descend to the greatest depths: since He is possessed of most, He can renounce most. And such a depth of condescension and self-renunciation on the part of God is actually taught us in the Holy Scriptures as the chief and fundamental article of the Christian faith and is presented in the strongest contrast to His majesty and glory as the greatest wonder of Divine love. God has been manifested in the flesh; the Son of God has become man; the Divine nature has condescended to assume the human and has been united to it in one person, in Jesus Christ—what can be more surprising, more worthy of admiration? In fact, if the Divine immensity, infinity, and glory displayed in the structure of the universe excite profound astonishment, this sentiment must be still further deepened when we behold Infinity voluntarily becoming finite for us, the unlimited for our sakes contracted within the narrow bounds of humanity, and the Lord of glory descending to a state of poverty and humiliation—without ceasing, however, to be in essence glorious, infinite, and illimitable.

All nature furnishes proofs that God is equally mighty and wonderful in the minute and in the great, on earth and in heaven, and that as nothing is too vast, so nothing is too little for Him. The microscope reveals the wonders of God's power as much as the telescope. If the manifestation of God's greatness and glory were confined to the starry heavens, He would be very mighty but not almighty. But He can be, and is, alike great and little, infinite and finite, high and low, Lord and servant.

Such are the representations of the Bible, which unveils the complete greatness and fullness in height and depth both of the power and of the love of God. However highly and gloriously it exalts Him above us, in the same degree does it bring Him down to the deepest recesses of our hearts. It is this Inspired Volume which first makes Him the object of our confidence and love, whilst the contemplation of God, simply as "the High and Holy One, Who inhabiteth eternity," awakens only emotions of astonishment and awe. In the latter case He remains at a strange distance from our hearts, sheds no heavenly consolation on our forlorn earthly existence, and grants no redemption from our sin and guilt. It was only such a heartless, lofty, distant deity Whom the poet before-mentioned (Schiller) had in his conceptions, when he sung of the gods of Greece, and with great justice—in opposition to the unchristian, unfeeling philosophy of his times—mourned over a desecrated, God-forsaken world. His lamentations would have been checked, had he known and acknowledged Him Who was both Son of God and Son of man, the Incarnate Deity, Who united heaven and earth, height and depth, in life and love with each other for ever; and of Whom Luther sings:

In our poor flesh and blood
The Eternal Good arrayed himself.

The intense craving of humanity after an intimate union and communication with the Eternal Godhead—which pervaded the whole heathen world, but in the absence of the light of revelation sought for satisfaction in gloomy dreams, in erroneous and immoral illusions—receives satisfaction in Christianity alone, consistently with purity and truth and in a manner worthy of God.

I wish to make the principal subject of my lectures the

Incarnation of the Deity in the person of Jesus Christ, which is the central point of the Christian system and the leading theme of the whole Bible. We would explore this "great mystery of godliness," as it is styled by Paul (1 Tim. 3:16), as far as the Scriptures reveal it. We shall in the first place endeavor to make some remarks on the nature of this wonderful union of the Divinity and the humanity in Jesus Christ, both in His humiliation to death, even the death of the cross, and in His exaltation at the right hand of the Father. Secondly, we shall state the reason and design of this event and the method by which it operates for our benefit.

It seems scarcely possible that anyone can contemplate without emotion an object at once so sublime and coming so closely in contact with ourselves. The overflowing love and mercy which distinguishes this deepest condescension of the Godhead is peculiarly calculated to move every heart. The astonishing combination of opposite qualities in Christ—the union of Divine majesty with the form of a servant, His elevation and His humiliation, His glory and His deep suffering—might arouse the dullest mind.

My lectures will naturally form a counterpart to those of the preceding year, since they will exhibit Him Whom we then recognized as seated on the circle of the heavens bringing Himself within the narrow confines of humanity; thus they will place in close connection the theology of the stars and the theology of the cross and show the points of harmony as well as of contrast. It is the same God here as there—above the stars, or under the cross; the same Lord, to Whom belongs all power in heaven and earth, with only this difference: that here, for the sake of the poor and debased, He threw over his garment of celestial light the mean raiment of poverty through which, nevertheless, to prove that its splendor was not extinguished but only concealed, the rays of Divinity beamed forth from time to time in His miracles and in the Transfiguration on Tabor. Therefore, in proportion as we admire the greatness of God's might and majesty in the starry heavens, must we praise the greatness of His goodness and mercy, which prompted Him to humble Himself for us creatures of the dust and to take upon Himself our poverty. Thus David felt, when in the eighth Psalm he says, *"When I consider Thy heavens, the work of Thy fingers, the moon and the stars which Thou hast ordained, what is man, that Thou art mindful of him? And the son of man, that Thou visitest him?"* We would in like manner be led from the contemplation of the stars, to the consideration of that Divine love which has been so gloriously illustrated in the Incarnation of the Son of God. For although He was "in the form of God, and thought it not robbery to be equal with God, yet He made Himself of no reputation and took upon Him the form of a servant, and was made in the likeness of men; and being found in fashion as a man, He humbled himself and became obedient unto death, even the death of the cross. Wherefore God also hath highly exalted Him, and given Him a name which is above every name, that at the name of Jesus every knee should bow, and that every tongue should confess that Jesus Christ is Lord, to the glory of God the Father." This passage presents the subject which we shall endeavor to explain in the next lecture.

2

UNION OF THE DIVINITY AND HUMANITY

ON THE UNION OF THE DIVINITY AND HUMANITY OF CHRIST.

ACCORDING to the plan laid down in the preceding lecture, we shall first make some remarks on the nature of this wonderful union of Divinity and humanity in Christ Jesus.

In precise terms, the doctrine may be thus expressed: THE SON OF GOD HAS ASSUMED HUMAN NATURE INTO THE UNITY OF HIS PERSON—a short proposition, which on account of its depth and richness of meaning demands a fuller consideration. And first let us inquire what we are to understand by the terms, "Son of God", "God the Father", and "God the Son". Are they founded on a mere human relation, which is applied only metaphorically to God without expressing anything really existing in the Deity? Such is the opinion of many in reference to this and similar subjects, but it is certainly an erroneous judgment, for while it presupposes that the Scriptures represent the relations of God to His creatures under human images, it forgets that human relations are formed according to the Divine image, for God created man in His own image. If God be altogether and perfectly love, He must communicate Himself entirely, without any reservation. But this is impossible towards created beings: they are too little, too contracted, too feeble to be recipients of the whole fullness of the Godhead. They can sustain the brightness of only a few sparks and scintillations of the Divine glory; its full and unmitigated splendor would be to them "a consuming fire", and hence they cannot be adequate objects for the everlasting and infinite love of God; the necessary limitation of their nature forbids it. God alone can be great enough for God. The eternal Father can admit to His full communion no being of less dignity than the eternal Son. Wherefore there existed with God the Father from all eternity, through His almighty power and love, God the Son, Who yet is not another God, but through Him is partaker of the same Divine essence, which the Father possessed from all eternity. For there is and can be only one Divine essence; the one indivisible Godhead belongs to the Father and the Son, and, through both, to the Holy Spirit.

Without involving ourselves in the depths of speculation on the doctrine of the Trinity, we may satisfy ourselves with a simple appeal to the Holy Scriptures.

"In the beginning was the Word," thus St. John's Gospel commences, "and the Word was with God, and the Word was God. All things were made by Him; and without Him was not anything made that was made" (Jn. 1:1, 3). In the epistle to the Colossians, the Son is called "the image of the invisible God, the first-born of every creature; for by Him were all things created that are in heaven and that are in earth, visible and invisible; and He is before all things, and by Him all things consist"; and, "In Him dwelleth all the fulness of the Godhead bodily." In the Epistle to the Hebrews the Son is denominated "the brightness of God's glory and the express image of His person, upholding all things by the Word of His power," as the Lord Himself declares in Matthew 28:18: "All power is given unto Me in heaven and in earth." But for proof that the Son is one God with the Father, Christ Himself says: "I and My Father are one" (Jn. 10:30), and "He that hath seen Me hath seen the Father" (Jn. 14:9); as also in John 17:10: "And all Mine are Thine, and Thine are Mine"; and in John 17:23: "That all men should honor the Son, even as they honor the Father." This would be sinful idolatry if the Son and the Father were not essentially equal and one.

It is therefore evident that there is a Son of God, Who through the Father is equal to the Father Himself in the might, honor, and majesty of the Godhead and is the eternal object of His supreme and entire love. He is, with the Father in the fellowship of the Holy Ghost, the one, true, eternal God.

The leading doctrine of Holy Writ is the fact that the everlasting Son of God has become man, and that, too, in an ascertained historical personage, namely, in Jesus of Nazareth, the Son of the Virgin Mary. The evangelist John in the introduction to his Gospel briefly touches on the existence of the eternal creative Word, the Fountain of all light and life, almost as an acknowledged truth. But in John 1:14, he brings forward his leading position and says: "The Word was made flesh and dwelt among us, and we beheld His glory, the glory as of the only-begotten of the Father, full of grace and truth." This great heart-elevating fact he never loses sight of throughout his Gospel, but by all the discourses and actions of Jesus therein narrated he aims to prove that this same Jesus was the Word manifested in the flesh, the incarnate God and Savior of the world, as he expressly declares in John 20:31: "These are written, that ye might believe that Jesus is the Christ, the Son of God, and that believing ye might have life through His name." And this is the leading proposition not merely of one Gospel, but of the whole New Testament, or rather of the whole Bible.

The whole of the Old Testament is a progressive series of preparatives, pre-intimations, and prophecies relative to the appearance of the Son of God among the people of Israel. Prophecy, beginning with general intimations, developed itself by declarations which continually became more full and specific. The Evangelist of the Old Testament (as Isaiah has often been called) speaks in the most express terms of the Virgin's Son: "Unto us a Child is born, unto us a Son is given: and the government shall be upon His shoulder: and His name shall be called Wonderful, Counsellor, The Mighty God, The Everlasting Father, The Prince of Peace" (Isa. 9:6). In contrast to this sublime description of His glory, he depicts the Messiah's state of humiliation and suffering in terms which can only apply to Jesus the Crucified (Isa. 53). The other prophets also mention various characteristics which meet in that Jesus of Whom Peter says, "To Him give all the prophets witness" (Acts 10:43). And while *they* testify of Him as *to come,* all the evangelists and apostles testify of Him as having come and dwelt among them, according to their uniform declarations both in the Gospels and in the Epistles: Jesus is the Christ, the Messiah, the Son of the living God, to Whom "all power is given in heaven and earth," and "in Whom all the families of the earth are blessed." Paul expressly calls Him, "God over all, blessed forever" (Rom.

9:5); and John at the close of his first epistle declares in the most explicit terms that Jesus Christ "is the true God and eternal life" (1 Jn. 5:20).

It is therefore not human nature in general but an historically-defined, specially-appointed individual, with Whom the God-head in the person of the Son has been united, and Who in consequence has become the Fountain of salvation for all men. In proportion to the immense disparity between God and man, especially when we consider the circumstances of ignominy and humiliation in which the man Jesus passed His life of poverty till it ended in His dying on the cross, is it necessary that we should form the worthiest and most correct conceptions of this union agreeably to the representations of Scripture. For without due care that which would tend to God's highest praise may easily be perverted to a contrary purpose: the truth, purity, and spirituality of the Divine Being may be denied, and instead of man being made after the image of God, a God may be fashioned after the image of man. In order to avoid falling into such a dangerous error, let us make one or two remarks by way of caution and explanation.

First. The Incarnation of the Son of God in Jesus Christ is not a necessary result of the constitution of the Divine nature but a free act of the Divine mercy and condescension. Were the former the case, it would prove that the Godhead was restricted through an absolute condition of its very being by what is finite and material, by time and space; that it was unavoidably contracted within the narrow limits of the earthly and necessarily brought down to the human form and nature. But let the absolute independence and infinity of God be thus given up, and the pure, unmixed simplicity of His spiritual nature is at once denied and His peerless perfection is reduced to human imperfection—in other words, His true Godhead is disowned and degraded.

But the Incarnation assumes altogether a different aspect, and what would be unworthy of the Godhead under the former supposition becomes worthy in the highest degree, as soon as we view it as an act of voluntary condescension. The same principle holds good in human conduct. It is thought unworthy of one who has reached maturity habitually to indulge in the sports and employments of childhood; it would be doing violence to the state of his faculties and the arrangements of the Creator. But it is esteemed most worthy and commendable in a parent or teacher, from the free impulse of love, to lower Himself down to the language and conceptions of His children or pupils in order to give them pleasure or to lead them onwards to a higher state of mental cultivation. Indeed this is the only way in which education can be properly conducted, as Luther admirably remarks: "Let no one think to show his sense by despising children's pursuits: Christ, in order to train men, found it needful to become man; and if we would train our children, we must also become children with them." In this beautiful passage Luther makes use of the doctrine under discussion and the sentiment is confirmed by the apostle, when he says: "Forasmuch then as the children are partakers of flesh and blood, He also himself likewise took part of the same" (Heb. 2:14). It is true that the difference and distance between God and men is infinitely greater than between men arrived at maturity and children; hence the Divine condescension manifested in the Incarnation reaches to a depth far beyond the ability of men adequately to conceive, and still more to imitate. On the other hand it should not remain unnoticed that the love of God, Who is Love itself, is so much the greater;

and it is the distinguishing property of this love, as it has no object above itself to love, to descend to the abject, the little, and the mean—not because they are so deserving of love, but because it is so compassionate. This is expressed in Psalm 113:5-7: "Who is like unto the Lord our God, Who humbleth Himself to behold the things that are in heaven, and in the earth? He raiseth up the poor out of the dust, and lifteth the needy out of the dunghill." And such is the language of the whole Bible, for Divine revelation both in the Old and the New Testament is nothing else than a continual exhibition of the Divine condescension, which reached its lowest depth in the Incarnation and especially in the last sufferings of the Savior. Throughout the Inspired Volume this love of the Most High presents itself to our notice, and amidst all the sublimity of the Divine majesty it speaks to men with the accents of humanity. We behold it choosing the oppressed race of Abraham, the despised people of Israel, as the depository of its revelations and glorifying itself in their midst by signs and wonders (Deut. 4:32; 7:7). Unless we keep in remembrance the condescending mercy of God, the great aim of the Holy Scriptures can never be understood. The vain deriders of the Bible know it not; and since they ignorantly suppose that the Bible represents that to be essential to the Divine Being, which is merely the effect of his condescension and free mercy, they have presumed to call the scriptural representations of God contracted and childish. But this only proves that in their unenlightened state they have no perception of the fulness and greatness of that Divine love which pities the human race with a mother's tenderness, and instead of allowing itself to be kept at a distance from them by their littleness, weakness, and impurity, constantly attends them with its holy loving-kindness.

Second. But we must not, in maintaining the doctrine of the Incarnation of the Son of God, forget the reality and essential immutability of His Divine nature. The Incarnation is not to be considered as a transmutation of the Divinity into the humanity, either in whole or in part. It would be false and degrading to say that the Divinity, which is incapable of deterioration or change, at a certain time ceased to be itself and began to be something else; that it gave up the possession of all or even of one of its attributes and exchanged its Divine essence for that of some other being or modified it by means of that other. To maintain this would be to reject altogether the true Divinity of the Son of God, for we should deny His essence to be eternal and immutable, which would be equivalent to denying it altogether. It would also be entirely opposed to the Holy Scriptures, for the passages we have mentioned above—"I and My Father are one"—"He that hath seen Me hath seen the Father"—"All men should honor the Son, even as they honor the Father," and another passage in Matthew 11:27: "All things are delivered unto Me of My Father"—are all spoken of our Lord in His state of humiliation. Neither could He be a true propitiation for our sins, unless real Divinity and real humanity were united in him.

But it may be asked: Wherein did His humiliation and self-renunciation consist, if He never ceased to be truly God? And are there not other passages which prove, that He surrendered perfect Divinity, as, for example, "My Father is greater than I" (Jn. 14:28; Mk. 13:32)? Is not also the same point proved by His whole human life and especially His last sufferings, under the load of which He cried out, "My God, My God, why hast Thou forsaken Me?" and a little time before: "My soul is exceeding sorrowful, even unto death"?

It may suffice to answer this objection by remarking, first, that the reality of the Divine nature does not destroy the reality of the human nature from which these expressions proceeded, as will be more fully shown in the course of our inquiry; and, secondly, that the Son of God in His state of humiliation certainly did abstain from the perfect use, the unlimited activity and transcendent glory of His Divine nature, but did not give up the possession of its essential properties. Without such abstinence the depth of the Divine condescension, self-denial, and self-renunciation—especially the reality of the Divine Incarnation, and along with that the true redemption and reconciliation of men—would be nullified. We must therefore contend for it earnestly, but it by no means follows that there was an essential change in His Divinity or its attributes.

An illustration may make this plain to us: the human eye when fully opened sees heaven and earth, when turned downward sees less, and when closed sees nothing at all; and yet in neither case does it suffer any change in its essential properties. Thus also His Divinity did not change its essence when it drew the veil of flesh over the beams of its glory. We must therefore adore it in the human nature of Jesus as truly Divine.

3

ON THE TRUE HUMANITY OF CHRIST

ON THE TRUE HUMANITY OF CHRIST, AND ITS PERSONAL UNION WITH THE GODHEAD.

To the observations made in the last Lecture we must add two others, in order to complete our view of the subject. We remark then, *Thirdly,* that in maintaining the doctrine of the Incarnation of the Son of God we must not lose sight of the truth and reality of His human nature. The union of the Divinity with the humanity in the person of Jesus is a fact so unique and extraordinary that to many persons it has seemed impossible, excepting on the supposition of an essential change in the humanity. Some indeed imagined that He had never been a real man, but only apparently so, having merely worn the mask of human form. Others, on the contrary, while they allowed that He had a real body, supposed that the indwelling Divinity supplied the place of a human soul. Others again have asserted that the human nature was changed and merged in the Divine—an error which not only denies the true humanity of the Redeemer, but also obscures and debases His Divinity by a mixture with what is heterogeneous and material. All these errors deprive the Redeemer of His relationship to us and participation of our nature, estrange Him from us, remove Him far out of our reach, and destroy His fitness for the work of mediation and propitiation, since they make Him related to only one of the two parties who are to be reconciled—that is, to God but not to men. They are also opposed to the whole tenor of Holy Writ, which everywhere, and particularly in the Gospels, represents our Lord as a real man. Though His conception was supernatural, and He soon gave proofs of being the Son of God, yet on His first appearance in this world, He was really a child Who grew in years and in wisdom (Lk. 2:40). He advanced to manhood in dutiful subjection to His parents; He ate and drank, He slept and wept and was made in all things like unto His brethren (Heb. 2:17) and "was in all points tempted like as we are, yet without sin" (4:15), for He was "holy, harmless, undefiled, and separate from sinners" (7:26). His participation of our nature was especially shown by the sufferings He endured. In the days of His flesh He "offered up prayers and supplications with strong crying and tears unto Him that was able to save Him from death, and was heard in that He feared; though He were a Son, yet learned He obedience, by the things which He suffered" (5:7, 8). His sufferings were truly human and caused Him to feel the deepest sorrows of which our nature is susceptible. His connection with the Divinity, so far from moderating, rendered them more intense, since it imparted an elevated perception and sympathy far above the sphere of ordinary humanity. In those sorrows which He endured on account of sin, He sympathized with the collective misery of the sinful human race. Under the overpowering influence of this exquisite sensibility, His human nature so full of tenderness wrestled in the severest agony in Gethsemane. His soul bowed itself in the dust and was exceeding sorrowful even unto death. His lips quivered at the bloody cup of suffering, which nevertheless, with meek and patient submission, He drank up. And when He was oppressed and afflicted, and the last deadly conflict of expiring humanity seized the Son of God, He sent forth with concentrated anguish the cry, "My God, my God, why hast Thou forsaken Me!" and death soon divided for a time the vital connection of the Divine nature with the body of Jesus. This serves to prove how great and real were the sufferings of His human nature in which also the Divine nature, though unaltered in its essence, took a share without being essentially affected thereby, in like manner as the soul of a dying man is sensible of death without dying itself.

The *fourth* and last remark we have to make is the following: as we must not confound together the Divinity and humanity in Jesus but let each subsist in its reality, so we must not separate them from one another, but view them continually as united personally or joined together in one consciousness. The ancient fathers have thus expressed it: the Divine and human natures are united in the person of Jesus, unmixed and unchanged, indissolubly and perpetually.

There are two dangerous rocks on which men may founder in reference to this important truth. Erroneous teachers have not been wanting, some of whom on the one, and some on the other, have suffered shipwreck, while the Church, holding the true faith and guided by the compass of Scripture, has steered between these uninjured. In the very endeavor to hold fast the unity of Christ's person, men have been led to confound the two natures, and while aiming to hold fast the reality of the two natures, they have insensibly been led to a separation of them, so as to attribute to the Man Jesus and to the Son of God an independence of one another, which reduces the connection to an inspiration, differing only in degree from that possessed by the prophets and apostles. This error also takes away the great source of consolation in Christ's Redemption and Atonement, which could not have been accomplished without a personal union of Divinity and humanity. A mere man by himself alone could as little redeem a world as he could create one, and though God by Himself alone can doubtless create, uphold, and govern the world, yet in order to redeem it, the union of the two divided parties is necessary, and a voluntary satisfaction for sin is required, which He alone can make Who at the same time stands *above* the Law and *under* the Law.

If we examine the Holy Scriptures, we shall find that the whole life of our Lord is marked by one personality, by a consciousness that was undivided, though varying in the extent of its operation. It is the same Being Who said, "My soul is exceeding sorrowful, even unto death," and, "All power is given unto Me in heaven and earth." He Who said, "The Son of man hath not where to lay his head," also declared that "all men should honor the Son, even as they honor the Father." It was the same Being Who on the cross exclaimed, "I thirst," and Who prayed, "Glorify me, Father, with the glory which I had with Thee before the world was."

Since we are neither to confound nor to separate the Divine and human natures in Jesus Christ, we cannot consider their mutual relation to be either more or less than a personal union. It is a unity of personal self-consciousness, which holds together and yet keeps separate the two natures; for in the Son of God there was a central point of consciousness of such a kind, that to the eternal consciousness of His Divine nature was added the temporal consciousness of His human nature—or rather, eternal Divine consciousness assumed to itself the human nature. This is expressed in the position which I laid down at the beginning of the second lecture: "The Son of God has assumed human nature into the unity of His person," that is, of His personal self-consciousness.

The Son of God has taken the human nature of Jesus into the unity of His person. This great act of God's condescension and mercy, we allow, will forever remain veiled in mysterious grandeur; yet thus much at least we may be able to discern, that it contains nothing impossible, contradictory, or unworthy of God, but that, on the contrary, it is most worthy of the Divine benevolence and agreeable to the truth and purity of the Supreme Being. The Son of God became a real man without ceasing to be truly God: wherefore we have now in Him (as it is declared in the Epistle to the Hebrews) "a great High Priest, that is passed into the heavens," and One Who is at the same time "touched with the feeling of our infirmities," since "He was in all points tempted like as we are, yet without sin" (Heb. 4:14, 15); "Forasmuch as the children are partakers of flesh and blood, He also himself likewise took part of the same," (2:14). He is God and man in one person; the Lord of heaven and earth, and yet our Brother and Kinsman; at the same time Creator and Creature; King and Servant; a Lion and a Lamb; almighty, and yet without might; glorious, and yet afflicted; the Prince of Life, and yet a Child of mortality. This is perfectly unique, extraordinary and wonderful. and indeed it must be so, for it is the noblest display of the Divine benevolence. But it involves no contradiction any more than when man in relation to his corporal and his spiritual nature is termed at once mortal and immortal, corruptible and incorruptible, temporal and eternal. The extraordinary blessings that accrue to the human race from this wonderful constitution of the Person of Christ, we shall consider in the sequel.

What then can human reason urge against the doctrine of the Incarnation of the Son of God or the Divinity of Jesus? Or on what grounds will it justify the sin of unbelief? This doctrine is supported by evidence so strong, so sacred, so overpowering, and is in itself so pure, glorious, and worthy of God that whether we consider the arguments addressed to our reason or the appeals made to our hearts, unbelief appears left without excuse. The Old and New Testaments verify it; all the prophets and apostles combined with the whole Christian Church have given it their united testimony, which confessors have sealed by their sufferings, and martyrs by their blood. In the midst of this sacred choir stands the Lord Himself in His humility and in His greatness, and so testifying of Himself both by His words and His works that the unbeliever must make Him a liar and regard Him either as an unparalleled deceiver or the most insane of visionaries. And how awful will be the guilt of him who can thus insult and reject the Savior of the world! What matchless fraud must unbelievers charge upon Him in Whose mouth was found no guile, if He falsely attempted to make the world believe that amidst all His outward poverty and meanness He was the Son of God; that He was to be the Ruler and Judge of the world; that they who had seen Him had seen the Father; and that all were bound to honor Him as they honored the Father. Or, if not chargeable with fraud, what wild insanity must they ascribe to Him Who in the most wretched outward condition could fancy Himself to be God and Lord. And of what outrageous folly and idolatry were His apostles and His followers in all subsequent ages guilty, to believe in Him and adore Him! But enough of such folly and impiety! No—what Scripture and the Church, what the Savior Himself with such ineffable holiness, wisdom, and humility, testified of Himself both by word and deed, must be true, or nothing is true, and it is unreasonable to believe anything. His Word *is* true, and "though heaven and earth should pass away," His Word shall not pass away. Let us only place His image, full of love and sanctity, before our eyes when He prayed to the Father, "Glorify Thou Me, Father, with the glory which I had with Thee, before the world was"; or when He declared to His disciples immediately before His Ascension, "All power is given unto me in heaven and earth"; or as He stood before the tribunal of the high priest, who, adjuring him by the living God, asked Him, "Art Thou the Christ, the Son of the Blessed?" and He answered, "I am"—and will not our hearts constrain us to confess, "Yes! Thou art—Thou art the Christ—the Son of the Blessed!"

Ask yourselves, is it possible to consider Him as a deceiver or a visionary and His first disciples and all Christians as dupes and fools? I say this not from an apprehension that any of such sentiments are to be found among you, but in order to point out into what absurdities and extravagances some men are led by that skepticism, which aims to subvert everything but establishes nothing—a skepticism which they are ready to extol as the pure solar light of reason and mental illumination, while it is in reality an irrational obscuration of the Divine light manifested to the world in Jesus Christ. The whole Christian Church reposes in the belief of Christ's Divinity: all Christian confessions abjure the denial of it as essentially anti-Christian. Amidst the many dissensions which have arisen in the Christian world, no error exists on this point, at least among the principal sections of the Church. The Roman Catholic, the Greek and Russian, the Lutheran, and the Reformed churches bear their independent, but unanimous testimony to the true Divinity and humanity of Jesus Christ: only a comparatively small number of men have relinquished this fundamental doctrine, which will forever remain the foundation and corner-stone of the temple of God.

There is only one consideration which can furnish any plausible ground for disbelieving this doctrine, and that is the consciousness of our own littleness, mean condition, and unworthiness, as well as the insignificance of our earth compared with the greatness of God and the vast extent of the universe. On these accounts the condescension of God in the Incarnation appears to many persons too great to be believed. The Almighty is too exalted, they imagine, to stoop so low. To obviate this objection, let me remind you of what I stated in the First Lecture, that to God nothing is too great or too little, and that He is equally worthy of admiration in the little and in the great, in depth as well as in height. Let us appeal to facts. Does nature around us indicate that our earth is neglected on account of its inconsiderable size compared with the universe of worlds around it? Are the smaller tribes of creatures on its surface formed with less care, with less exquisite adaptation of their parts, with scantier means of providing for their wants than the larger animals? Or rather, does not the minutest insect, the smallest bird, the most delicate flower furnish the most cogent and delightful evidence that the gracious providence of God extends to even the least and most inconsiderable individual of His creatures? Therefore let our earth be relatively ever so little, and man upon it ever so inconsiderable compared with higher orders of rational beings; yet we know from the Scriptures that though the Lord dwelleth on high, He hath respect to the lowly; and we shall not dare to allow a sense of our littleness to lead us to doubt the greatness of the Divine mercy, but shall only be prompted by it to the humble and joyful acknowledgment, "What is man, that Thou art mindful of him, and the son of man, that Thou visitest him?"

4

ON THE COMMUNION OF PROPERTIES

ON THE COMMUNITY OF PROPERTIES AND CONDITION BETWEEN THE DIVINE AND HUMAN NATURES IN CHRIST.

As we have now shown that in Christ two distinct natures, the Divine and the human, are united with each other in one inseparable person, an inquiry of the highest interest naturally arises, in what relation these two natures stand to each other; whether they are held in mutual connection by that one central point of consciousness to which we have adverted, while each of them retains, in an exclusive manner, its own properties and states; or whether, in consequence of this connection, each reciprocally partakes of the properties and states of the other. The latter we conceive must be maintained as a necessary consequence of the personal union of the two natures without mixture or transmutation. If no such reciprocal participation ensued, the Incarnation would be only a Divine contact with human nature in a single point without any real communion of the Divine and the human. But without such a communion, even if the contact should take place in more points than one, no reconciliation or redemption (in the proper and full sense of the word) could be effected, since the Divinity and the humanity, however near they might approach one another, would still remain disunited or divided; and the human nature, unless pervaded by the Divine, could never make satisfaction for the sins of the world.

We must ever bear in mind that the point of union to both natures is the central point of consciousness in which they co-center. Now this, as we have seen, stands in the most intimate connection with the essence of both, so that by means of this central point both natures are placed in the most intimate connection with one another. Hence it is that without confounding the two natures, such an intimate communion of the Divinity and humanity exists in Jesus that what properly belongs to the essence of the Divinity may be affirmed of the humanity, and what belongs to the essence of the humanity may be affirmed of the Divinity. From this wonderful combination of two natures so essentially distinct as the Divine and the human in the person of Jesus, several truths are deducible which will excite our wonder and admiration, the more accurately we apply them to the extraordinary circumstances of his life both before and after His crucifixion. In other words, to those events which occurred in His state of humiliation and in His state of exaltation. But however astonishing, they are not less important and salutary, elevating and consoling.

The first inference deducible from the combination of the two natures is this, that respecting the person in Whom they are united, opposite assertions can be made with equal propriety and without any real inconsistency. The whole person of the God-Man we are accustomed to designate by the appellation *Christ,* or *Mediator,* or *Lord*; the Divine nature by the name *Son of God*; and the human, by the name *Son of Man,* or *Jesus.* That which belongs peculiarly either to the Divine or the human nature can therefore be alike asserted with perfect truth of Christ or the Mediator, as we find, for instance, in Luke 21:26, "Ought not Christ to have suffered these things, and to enter into His glory?" In Him Divine glory and the form of a servant, the highest dignity and the deepest humiliation, almighty power and finite weakness, heavenly honor and earthly dishonor, infinite riches and extreme penury, strangely meet, as it is expressed in another passage, "Though He was rich, yet for our sakes He became poor, that we through His poverty might be made rich" (2 Cor. 8:9). That no real opposition exists in the qualities thus contrasted we have shown on a former occasion. How wonderful and impressive is the contemplation of this combination of divers excellences in the great Mediator; His gentleness and His greatness; His submission and His power; His lowliness and His exaltation; His having nothing, and yet possessing all things!

The second consequence of the personal union of the Divinity and humanity in Jesus is that by means of this central consciousness the Divine nature is susceptible of the qualities of humanity without any alteration in its own essence. The Divinity does not become in itself weak or needy, or passible, but it becomes personally conscious, through its union with the humanity, what it is to be poor and weak, to suffer pain and to die. It has thus a real fellow-feeling and sympathy, so beautifully expressed by the apostle (Heb. 4:15, 7) when he says, "We have not a High Priest Who cannot be touched with the feeling of our infirmities; but Who was tempted in all points as we are, yet without sin," and, "Although He were a Son, yet learned He obedience by the things He suffered." The communication of human suffering to the Divinity is something so extraordinary and singular that no language can furnish adequate expressions by which to describe the effect which the belief of this truth produces on the heart. In fact, an awful shuddering must pass through our inmost soul when we think of "crucifying the Lord of glory" (1 Cor. 2:8). That the Son of God—the true, eternal God—was scourged, spit upon, tortured to death, is amazing, is overwhelmingly awful. And the awfulness of the thought is in nowise diminished by the consideration that those intense sufferings were inflicted on the human, and not on the Divine nature; for we have already seen that since both are connected in one person, the states of the one are through a common consciousness participated by the other. Let me refer again to the illustration presented in the union of body and soul. If the body be in pain, does not the whole person feel it? Does not the soul really and truly sympathize with it? And when the body dies, does not the soul undergo the pains and sufferings of death? Thus it was with the Redeemer: the Divinity, immortal and impassible in itself, nevertheless being connected with the humanity, felt its suffering and dying as its own. For in consequence of the Incarnation, all that belonged to the Man Jesus became its own, though without any change in its essence, so that the apostle Paul did not hesitate to say, "Feed the Church of God, which He hath purchased with His own blood" (Acts 20:28). We cannot, therefore, conceal the fact but must allow it to stand before us in all its awfulness, that God has suffered in Jesus, that He was dishonored and treated ignominiously by His creatures, that He bore the cross, that He felt the pains and torture of crucifixion, and experienced the dread of death common to humanity. This is an awful spectacle, we allow; but let us not on that account turn away from it, for it is as consoling as it is awful. Our Lord might, indeed, have avoided all these sufferings. "Thinkest thou not"—these are His own words—"that I could have prayed the Father, and He would have sent me more than twelve legions of angels?" (Matt. 26:53). It was on His part a voluntary subjection to ignominy and suffering for our sakes that in the midst of suffering, distress, and death we might enjoy consolation and evince patience, upheld by the grace and peace of God. There is nothing which more tends to make us faithless towards God, to deprive us of the consolatory feeling of His love, and to render us insensible of His beneficent presence, than suffering, distress, and death, especially when the thorns and thistles in our paths are sharpened (as must be the case with guilty mortals) by the consciousness of our sins and manifold transgressions. We feel ourselves at a distance from God, destitute of His love and peace and consequently harassed, restless, and tormented, full of discontent and pain, and often on the borders of despair. In order that our corporeal and spiritual ills might no longer separate us from Him and thus lead to irretrievable ruin, God has Himself endured them. That the cross might no longer alienate us from Him and completely overwhelm us, He has in His assumed humanity borne it and allowed Himself to be fastened to it. Thus He enables us to "take up our cross and follow Him," and, supported by our communion with Him, to overcome pain, sorrow, and death, and to meet without trembling that enemy, the great accuser who "has the power of death." What sacredness is now impressed on all earthly sufferings by the holy sufferings of the Son of God! The griefs of mortality seem almost Divine when we think of His sorrows. What honor has the lowly form of a servant which He assumed imparted to poverty and meanness! How gentle and peaceful has His death rendered ours! God has suffered; out of abundant grace and compassion He has suffered as man, and blotted out our sins. This is a balsam whose virtues can assuage the severest pains; this is consolation which enters our inmost souls and becomes the foretaste and pledge of immortal joys.

It is indeed the duty of finite beings to bow before the unsearchable wisdom of God, and submit themselves to its decrees; but if, while we are oppressed by sorrow and gloom, we contemplate God only as enjoying in Himself heavenly and everlasting rest and surrounded with His transcendent and essential glory, we obtain no satisfaction adequate to sweeten the bitterness of grief and to pour Divine peace into our troubled hearts. How vastly different an effect is produced by a sense of that unfathomable love—that inexhaustible sympathy, which caused the great and glorious God to descend to a participation of our sufferings, in order that we, being reconciled to Him, might be raised to a participation of His glory! As the apostle Paul says, "If so be we suffer with Him, that we may also be glorified together" (Rom. 8:17).

But let us not merely contemplate sufferings; let us survey the whole of human life. Has not the whole of human existence and life with all its duties, from birth even to death—has not human nature, both body and soul, been sanctified, ennobled, and rendered divine, by the holy indwelling of the Divinity in the Man Jesus? He was made, as we know, like ourselves in all points, sin excepted; He assumed our flesh and blood, which are the same in all men; He became in this respect one of our race—our relation, our brother. Whatever, therefore, in and through Him has been imparted to the human race, of that we all partake. Should we not, therefore, deem it an honor and a motive for holy joy that all that we have and are—our exercises of thought, will, and feeling, our bodily senses and members, our acting and resting, our waking and sleeping, our eating and drinking, our childhood, our youth, and our riper age—in short, our whole life from birth even to death, has been brought through Jesus Christ into so near and intimate a connection with the Godhead? Has not our little earth been sanctified, glorified, and consecrated as a temple of God, since the Most High hath condescended so far as to walk upon it in human form and as a citizen of earth to live and suffer on its soil? Who is there that would not now rejoice with a sentiment of far deeper gratitude, that He belongs to the human race? And ought not all who bear the Christian name to exult in the words of Moses: "What nation is there so great, who hath God so nigh unto them, as the Lord our God is in all things that we call upon Him for?"

The truth of these observations will appear still more evident if we consider a third consequence which results from the personal union of the Divinity and humanity in Jesus Christ. It is this—that by means of the consciousness common to both, the properties of the Divine nature are joined to the human nature, yet without passing over into its essence. In proportion to the depth of the Divine condescension is the height to which our nature has been raised. In common life if there be any relation founded on love between the stronger and the weaker, between the superior and the inferior, the latter cannot fail to be elevated and strengthened by the former. Thus in the case of parents and children we see strength upholding weakness, wisdom guiding ignorance, ability aiding incapacity. The personal union of the

Divine and human natures in Jesus Christ is the most intimate, without transmutation, that can exist, and that, too, between the Almighty and fallen man—between the Most High and a worm of the dust. How otherwise was it possible that the human nature, though in essence unaltered, obtained in consequence of that union capability, knowledge, and effective energy to a degree infinitely beyond any mere man, however distinguished? Through the Divine omnipotence it displayed at pleasure an ability far beyond human power. Hence the winds and waves obeyed the command of Jesus; at His bidding the dead arose, the blind saw, the lame walked, and the dumb spoke. Through the Divine omniscience, the human intelligence of Jesus was so heightened that it could be affirmed, "He needed not that any should testify of man, for He knew what was in man" (Jn. 2:25). Through the Divine omnipresence it was possible for Him to be wherever He willed, as He Himself declares in Matthew 18:20: "Wherever two or three are gathered together in My name, there am I in the midst of them." This glorification of human nature was already manifested before the death of Jesus in His state of humiliation, though in a degree vastly inferior to their manifestation after His resurrection and ascension. In His state of exaltation the human nature was raised, glorified, and refined: it entered into a much closer, more exalted, and intimate participation of the Divine attributes than was possible on earth when confined within the bounds of space and time. The humanity of Jesus in intimate connection with the Divinity now rules over all things with Divine supremacy, as St. Paul declares, "that at the name of Jesus every knee must bow" (Phil. 2:10); this also Stephen implied when He prayed, "Lord Jesus, receive my spirit!" (Acts 7:58).

If we compare this our third inference with the preceding, it will appear that the elevation of the humanity to the Divinity and the descent of the Divinity to the humanity perfectly correspond to each other, and that consequently the two natures are introduced into the nearest and most intimate alliance. Whilst by the contemplation of the Divinity assuming humanity our hearts are softened and comforted, they are filled with joyful elevation on beholding the humanity taken into fellowship with the Divine glory. I would here repeat that of what our Elder Brother possesses essentially or by direct communication from the Divinity, we shall each of us receive a portion, through His mediation, corresponding to the degree of our faith and love in Him: that which is His by nature will be ours through grace (Jn. 17:22). How may we exult in the dignity conferred upon us all, that one of our race is exalted even above angels and seated at the right hand of the Most High, and that "at His name every knee must bow, of things in heaven, and things in earth, and things under the earth!" What an honor has been conferred on the female sex that one of their number has given birth to Him Who is the Lord of the world! What confidence should it impart to every heart that a King reigns over the universe Who is God and man in one person and Whose compassion and love to our race are not less than His glory and power!

The true dignity of man consists not so much in his possession of reason and free-will (for these he has in common with evil spirits) as in his close connection and communion with God. It consists not in what we have acquired for ourselves but in what God has given us. When a man is proud of himself—of his dignity, talents, and virtues—and imagines himself by his own merit to be something in the sight of God and his fellow-creatures, his boasting is the pride of a beggar and has the foul taint of self-love. We may with truth call this a creature of the imagination, for it is only a false image which man forms of himself, and having adorned it with the colors of self-love he becomes enamored with it. But God, Who created us after His own image, rejects the false images we have formed of ourselves; He shows us in the mirror of His Law the stains of sin; takes off the gaudy colors by which we attempt to conceal our real deformity, and thus convinces us how little we have the image of God; that in His sight we are wretched sinners—creatures of the dust, and worms of the earth. The greatness and magnificence of the universe around us display still more our littleness and poverty: "Behold, even the moon it shineth not, yea, the stars are not pure in His sight; how much less man that is a worm, and the son of man, which is a worm" (Job 25:5, 6). Thus no flesh can glory before Him, but he who would glory must glory in the Lord, as Mary expresses it in her beautiful song of praise: "My soul doth magnify the Lord, and my spirit rejoiceth in God my Savior; for He hath regarded the low estate of his handmaiden" (Luke 1:46); or as it is declared by the Psalmist: "The Lord hath done great things for us, whereof we are glad." Let this be our joy, our delight, our glory: that the Lord hath looked on our forlorn condition, that He hath descended so low to us His sinful children and hath exalted us so near Himself. Through His mercy the human has become Divine, and the Divine has become human; through His loving-kindness, the children of men have become the sons of God. What more can we desire than to have God for our Father and the Son of God for our Elder Brother, through Whom heaven and earth are ours, as the Apostle says: "All are yours, and ye are Christ's, and Christ is God's" (1 Cor. 3:22)? I close, therefore, with the words of the prophet: "'Let not the wise man glory in his wisdom; let not the rich man glory in his riches; but let him that glorieth, glory in this: that he understandeth and knoweth Me, that I am the Lord, which exerciseth loving-kindness, judgment, and righteousness in the earth; for in these things I delight,' saith the Lord" (Jer. 9:23).

5

STATES OF HUMILIATION AND OF EXALTATION

ON CHRIST'S STATE OF HUMILIATION AND OF EXALTATION.

We have now to consider more attentively the two states of our Lord, namely, His state of humiliation and His state of exaltation. Each of these is divided into successive steps or stages: the first descending to the lowest depths, and the second ascending to the heights of celestial glory. Let us present to your contemplation the gradations of each series.

The state of humiliation begins with the Incarnation, and its first stage is the lowly birth of the Savior in the manger at Bethlehem. He Who with the Father and the Holy Spirit is the true God from eternity lay as an infant in His mother's arms! Wonderful, unfathomable thought! That He Who was by nature so great should become so little out of love to us! Truly, this littleness and weakness is more astonishing than that greatness which sustains all worlds by its power. Divine love appeared in this world under the form of an innocent child. If all the poets on earth were to unite their powers, could they produce anything more engaging, more lovely, more touching than that which actually took place at Bethlehem in the land of Judea? There Divine Majesty laid aside its splendor; love divested itself of its brilliancy and power and disarmed eternal justice of its wrath against the sinner. God is love, but here love laid aside its superhuman majesty, made itself of no reputation, was found in the likeness of a child, received the caresses of a mother, and associated with children of its own age. The most excursive fancy can conceive nothing more tender, more beautiful, more heart-affecting than this, which, since it is no fancy, but truth, brings under a lowly form the richest consolation of Divine grace and imparts a heavenly sanctity to our poor human life, even in its earliest stages. The great masters of painting have taken, as the most beautiful subject for their art, Mary and her Divine Child. Certainly to minds of every class it is a most lovely and consoling image, but what more than all is calculated to excite the deepest emotion is the fact that this Divine Child from the very beginning of His earthly life was subjected to privation and persecution. Since it was His design to be the comforter of the poor and the distressed, He shunned neither poverty nor distress. No palace, but an inn, received Him at His birth; He was laid in no royal cradle, but in a manger. The tyrant Herod sought after His life but could not touch him, because He was the Son of God; and notwithstanding His poverty and mean condition, the shepherds and the wise men from the east did Him homage, and angels chanted their song of praise.

The second stage in the Savior's state of humiliation was His life of poverty and meekness in constant obedience to the

Law. Thus St. Paul says: "God sent forth His Son, made of a woman, made under the Law" (Gal. 4:4). The evangelist Luke informs us that He went with Joseph and Mary to Nazareth and "was subject unto them" (Lk. 2:51). The Lord of the world was subjected to human control: He obeyed His mother and assisted His supposed father in his occupation as a carpenter. He lived among the people of Nazareth as one of them without assuming any authority, though He was "strong in spirit" and "increased in wisdom and stature, and in favor with God and men" (Lk. 2:40, 52). The Lord of the Law became its servant and fulfilled its minutest requirements (Matt. 5:17). He submitted to circumcision and to all the righteousness of the Law and both by doing and suffering yielded to it a perfect obedience. Added to this, He lived in a condition of extreme poverty, for "though He was rich, yet for our sakes He became poor." The Son, Whom the Father, as the Scripture saith, "appointed heir of all things, by Whom also He made the worlds," had not in His own world "where He could lay His head" (Matt. 8:20). Instead of the blessed hosts of holy angels and exalted spirits who served and adored Him in His heavenly glory, He was surrounded by publicans and sinners, the blind and lame, the diseased and possessed. Men of rank, the rich and the learned, were offended at His low condition and received Him not. In short, by the world, his own possession, He was rejected, as St. John declares in the beginning of his Gospel: "He was in the world, and the world was made by Him, and the world knew Him not; but as many as received Him, to them gave He power to become the sons of God" (Jn. 1:10, 12).

The third step in Christ's humiliation was His suffering and dying: "He humbled himself," says the Apostle, "and became obedient unto death, even the death of the cross" (Phil. 2:8). "I am the good Shepherd," our Lord Himself declared; "the good Shepherd giveth His life for the sheep" (Jn. 10:11). And as He was going up to Jerusalem, the scene of his last sufferings, with His disciples, He said to them, "Behold, the Son of man shall be delivered unto the chief priests and unto the Scribes; and they shall condemn Him to death and shall deliver Him to the Gentiles: and they shall mock Him, and they shall scourge Him, and shall spit upon Him, and shall kill Him: and the third day He shall rise again" (Mk. 10:33, 34). We see from these passages how distinctly His sufferings were present to His Divine soul, and that He was impelled only by holy love to meet and endure a disgraceful and agonizing death for the salvation of the human race. It was the spontaneous determination of His love to submit to this depth of humiliation. "No man," said He, "taketh my life from me, but I lay it down of Myself. I have power to lay it down, and I have power to take it again" (Jn. 10:18). Armed with this Divine resolution, He readily went forth to the conflict with death and hell. As He drew near to Jerusalem, He shed tears of pity over the city where He was about to suffer, and entered it mild as a lamb, courageous as a lion. After celebrating the holy supper with His disciples, the hour of suffering began in Gethsemane: there He lay, prostrate in the dust, "troubled even unto death," and prayed: "'Father, if it be possible, let this cup pass from Me: nevertheless, not My will, but Thine, be done.'...And being in an agony He prayed more earnestly, and His sweat was as it were great drops of blood falling down to the ground" (Lk. 22:42, 44). How intense, how appalling must have been those sufferings! Surely far beyond the mere natural shrinking from approaching death. Jesus then felt in His Divine consciousness and sympathy the whole misery of the human race, whose sins He was to expiate; He felt the curse of the Law and the full weight and pressure of the Divine justice against that sinful world which He came to reconcile and redeem: "God was in Christ," says St. Paul, "reconciling the world unto Himself" (2 Cor. 5:19). Let us, therefore, whenever we contemplate the depth of those sufferings, at the same time recollect the super-eminent dignity of the Sufferer—that it was God Who in the assumed humanity reconciled the world unto Himself by that intensity of suffering. He was betrayed, bound, dragged before His judges, and condemned to the most ignominious death, the lot of none but the most abandoned criminals. The cross was erected on Golgotha, and the Lord of glory, an object of mockery and contempt, was affixed to it by piercing nails that He might shed His blood on the accursed tree as a sin-offering and obtain "eternal redemption" for the world. "Christ hath redeemed us from the curse of the Law, being made a curse for us; for it is written, 'Cursed is every one that hangeth on a tree'" (Gal. 3:13). Such was the humiliation of the Ever-Blessed and "Only-Begotten of the Father" that He was made a curse for the world and died an accursed death to save those who were under the curse. What immeasurable love! What unfathomable mercy! What depth of self-renunciation! Surely I am justified in asserting that the display of God's glory in the starry heavens is not so wonderful as the humiliation of Christ upon the cross. Whenever, therefore, you gaze with admiration on the brilliancy of the firmament as an exhibition of the Creator's glory, think also of the cross and of the supernatural darkness on Golgotha, in order rightly to apprehend the whole height and depth, the might and the mercy of our God. On the altar of the cross the Son completed the great sacrifice of Himself, amidst unutterable sufferings, and having prayed for sinners and commended His soul into His Father's hands, He bowed His head and expired. All nature mourned for its Lord; darkness covered the land; the earth trembled; the rocks were rent asunder; the centurion who guarded the cross, and they that were with him watching Jesus cried out in amazement, "Truly this was the Son of God!" (Matt. 27:54).

The fourth step in the Savior's humiliation was His burial and descent into hell. His body was deposited in the new tomb belonging to Joseph of Arimathea: there lay that body in which, as St. Paul says, dwelt "all the fullness of the Godhead bodily" (Col. 2:9). The corpse of Him Who was "Lord of lords and King of kings" slept the sleep of death in the bosom of the earth. Thus have our graves been hallowed by His tomb, and the vault of death has become a divine resting-place. But the Spirit of the Lord was not unemployed while His body was in the grave, but went, as Peter informs us and preached to the spirits in prison (1 Pet. 3:19).[1] The Lord of glory humbled Himself even to hell. But it was this lowest reach of humiliation which burst the bands of hell and broke the power of its chief, so that if we faithfully adhere to Christ, we have no cause to dread the deadly venom of that deceitful serpent on whose head He has trodden. And here let it be observed that the devil, as he is represented in the Scriptures, is not a mere phantom of superstition, but rather a crafty, aspiring spirit. The devil is for the most part described in the Scriptures not as a domineering spirit who accomplishes his aim by open force, but as a most dangerous tempter and enemy of souls, who governs all those who are not

---

1 Commentators have generally given a different interpretation to this passage. The word translated "hell," in our version of the Scriptures, sometimes denotes the *grave* (cf. Ps. 26:10 with Acts 2:27), or the invisible state (Rev. 1:18). Most commentators consider that Christ did not go to the place of torment.—Ed.

delivered by a spiritual, heartfelt communion with the Lord from the tyranny of sin, selfishness, and evil desires, which form Satan's congenial element. But Jesus Christ destroyed the works of this proud, malignant spirit by means of His own self-renouncing descent to death and hell, so that now a true Christian can boldly say, "O death, where is thy sting? O grave, where is thy victory? Thanks be to God, which giveth us the victory through our Lord Jesus Christ," Who descended as a mighty conqueror from heaven, through our world, to hell, and returned in triumph to the right hand of the Majesty on high, that He might fill all things with His holy presence, as Paul declares in Ephesians 4:10.

As the most important result of Christ's descent to hell was His victory and triumph over the dark infernal powers, it naturally leads us to consider that state of exaltation to which it forms the transition, and of which—according to the view of many divines—it is a constituent part. The last and lowest step of His humiliation is thus connected with the first of His exaltation, and the glorious, resplendent appearance of the latter forms a striking contrast to the sadness and gloom of the former. Connecting both of these in our view of the person of Christ, Who descended to such depths and rose so high, Who suffered so awfully and reigns so gloriously, I would ask once more: what can all fancy or poetry invent more sublime, more captivating, more elevating, and yet more humbling, than not the mere idea but the real person of Him Who was God and man, in Whose wonderful fullness we behold everything combined to move or to tranquillize the heart, to affect us with sorrow or joy, to alarm or to console? He Who, with the Father and the Holy Ghost, is the one God and Creator of the universe, upholding all things by the Word of His power, even He became a Child Who smiled on His mother's lap. He is the King of glory, before Whom the angelic host cast their crowns, and yet He was so despised and afflicted that men hid, as it were, their faces from Him. He is Lord of glory, clothed with the mantle of the stars, yet He was stripped and fastened to the cross, and instead of a celestial array only the nails and the crown of thorns and bloody wounds were to be seen. He is to be the Judge of the world, and yet was numbered by men among the transgressors. He dwelt in unapproachable light, receiving the homage and service of all holy spirits; but He also descended into the outer darkness, and the hosts of evil spirits fled from before His face. Again He ascended on high, and all creatures above and below must bow the knee and confess that He Who in the form of a servant humbled Himself unto death, even the death of the cross, is Lord of all. And when we are informed and assured that this glorious and wonderful Being, in Whom are met an assemblage of events and facts so strangely contrasted, performed and endured all this on our account, out of love to us, our hearts are overwhelmed with the thought: we attempt in vain to enter into the bitterness of that sorrow or the ineffable delight of that joy which filled the breast of the Redeemer; we are laid prostrate in the deepest emotion before the power of such amazing love and of such transcendent greatness. And surely if the heart has once been thus touched and visited, it can never more be disobedient to that King Who is so full of love and sympathy; it can never wander again from that good Shepherd Who refreshes the weary; it can never forsake that heavenly Friend any more than the bride can forsake the bridegroom.

But we must now turn to the consideration of the Savior's exaltation. The first step in this series is the Resurrection of the Lord. David prophesied of the Messiah: "Thou wilt not leave my soul in hell, neither wilt thou suffer thine Holy One to see corruption" (Ps. 16:10). Peter, referring to this prophecy, testified before all the Jews on the day of Pentecost: "Him Whom ye have taken, and by wicked hands have crucified and slain, God hath raised up, having loosed the pains of death, because it was not possible that He should be holden of it" (Acts 2:23, 24); and in the same manner he addressed the Gentiles in the name of all the apostles, telling them that God had raised up the crucified Jesus "on the third day, and showed Him openly, not to all the people, but unto witnesses chosen before of God, who did eat and drink with Him after He rose from the dead" (Acts 10:40, 41). On the morning of the third day our Lord burst the bands of death, broke the bars of the grave, and came forth from the sepulchre full of Divine power. The guards fled; the disciples refused to believe the women who had seen him, until He came himself into their midst with the salutation, "Peace be unto you." To convince them that He was not a disembodied spirit, He pointed to His pierced hands and feet and partook of food in their presence. But Thomas, who was not present at this interview, refused to credit the report of his brethren unless he could put his own finger into the print of the nails. The Lord appeared to this doubting one and invited him to thrust his hand into His side, exhorting him not to be faithless, but believing. Then said Thomas unto Him, "My Lord and my God!" Thus He proved himself by His resurrection, even to this incredulous disciple, to be his Lord and God; and we must with Thomas acknowledge "the Firstborn from the dead" as our Lord and God, Who will also awaken us from death and give unto us eternal life, for what belongs to Him must become ours also. And with Him, the Risen One, we already here below walk "in newness of life" (Rom. 6:4).

The second stage of Christ's exaltation is His Ascension, which is thus narrated by Luke: "And it came to pass, while He blessed them, He was parted from them, and carried up into heaven, and a cloud received Him out of their sight." Before this event, from the time the Savior rose from the dead, His body had become far more heavenly and spiritual than our gross and earthly bodies, as may be inferred from His appearing suddenly to His disciples and vanishing again before their eyes. This glorious alteration in the corporeal part of His nature was earned to a greater extent at His Ascension, though without affecting the essential qualities of His humanity. Our Lord at His Ascension, through His Divine power, was freed from the earth's attraction, and, borne away from the sphere of its influence, He ascended to heaven, the boundless residence of the ever-present God. He is not, however, removed to a distance from us or withdrawn to a portion of space remote from our world—on the contrary, He is now near to us in a manner that was before impossible. For as long as He was confined within the earthly limits of human nature, He could stay in only one fixed place, and could only slowly change His situation. But since He has been elevated beyond these limits, He can be everywhere present, wherever His disciples need His aid, and thus can fulfill His promise: "Lo, I am with you always, even unto the end of the world" (Matt. 28:20), and, "Where two or three are gathered together in My name, there am I in the midst of them" (Matt. 18:20). Hence we perceive that His Ascension contributes not only to His glory, but to our salvation; since we not only shall be exalted hereafter to participate in His glory (Jn. 17:24), but may be confident of enjoying even now the holy presence of Him Who "descended first into the lower parts of the earth," and then "ascended up far above all heavens, that He might fill all things," as St. Paul declares: "He ascended up on high; He led captivity captive, and gave gifts unto men!" (Eph. 4:8-10).

The third step in the Savior's exaltation is His Session at the right hand of God. It is thus recorded by the evangelist Mark: "So then, after the Lord had spoken unto them, He was received up into heaven, and sat on the right hand of God" (Mk. 16:19); and Paul declares that "the God of our Lord Jesus Christ, the Father of glory, set Him at His own right hand in the heavenly places, far above all principality, and might, and dominion, and every name that is named, not only in this world, but also in that which is to come; and hath put all things under His feet, and gave Him to be head over all things to the Church, which is His body, the fullness of Him that filleth all in all" (Eph. 1:17, 20-23). Similar language is used in the Old Testament: "The Lord said unto my Lord, 'Sit Thou at my right hand, until I make thine enemies thy footstool'" (Ps. 110:1). On this subject many persons imagine that they show superior discernment when they remark that the Divine Being, strictly speaking, has neither a right hand nor a left, nor a throne whereon any other being can sit beside Him. All this may be very true, but they are wrong in supposing that the expressions of Scripture are to be taken in an absolutely literal sense. The right hand of God in Scripture never means a particular place in heaven or in relation to the Divine Being, but is used to express the almighty power and sovereignty of God by which He governs all things. "To sit at the right hand of God" means to share in His government, as it is explained by St. Paul in the passage above quoted. By His Ascension to heaven the Son of God was again introduced into the unlimited use of his Divine attributes, and the glorified human nature of Jesus shared in His Divine majesty. In eternal, indissoluble connection with the Father and the Holy Spirit, the Mediator rules all things and protects His people against all their enemies. In His hands are all the arrangements of Providence and all our destinies. To whom could we entrust ourselves, and all we are and have, with such confidence as to Him Who is truly God with God, and as truly man with man, and Who exercises the tenderest sympathy towards all His brethren? Wherefore let us look "unto Jesus, the author and finisher of our faith; Who for the joy that was set before Him endured the cross, despising the shame, and is set down at the right hand of the throne of God" (Heb. 12:2). Let "our conversation be in heaven, from whence also we look for the Savior, the Lord Jesus Christ," (Phil. 3:20).

The fourth and last step in the exaltation of Christ is His coming again to Judgment. "The Son of Man"—these are His own words—"shall come in His glory, and all the holy angels with Him, then shall He sit upon the throne of His glory: and before Him shall be gathered all nations." The Son of God appeared once in the world in deep abasement and under the form of a servant; He will appear a second time in majesty and glory. Once He was Himself judged in weakness; but at His second coming He will judge the world in power. Each step in His state of exaltation has a corresponding step in His state of humiliation. His resurrection corresponds to His death and burial; His ascension, to His descent into hell; His session at the right hand of God, to His life of poverty and suffering; and His second coming, to His first advent in the flesh. The union of the most opposite qualities in the person of our Lord has been so often pointed out to you that it is less necessary for me to enlarge upon the astonishing contrast between His first and second coming. *There* He was seen as a poor infant in the manger, but *here* He will appear as the Lord of the hosts of heaven, and all the nations of the earth shall bow before Him. It will then be manifest to all the world that His first appearance among men was only a relinquishment or concealment of His Supreme Majesty for their salvation, and that, when exalted again to the invisible throne of the Godhead, He exercised His long-suffering for their conversion, till the day of grace had expired and the day of judgment had arrived. Then will the Divine majesty of the Son appear once more in His assumed humanity—not indeed in the lowly form of an infant or a servant, but with awful grandeur, in mighty power and glory, surrounded by ministering angels, and refulgent with the splendor of immortality. *When* that hour will arrive no one knoweth, for the Father hath reserved it in His own power, but whenever it may be, it will lay the world in ruins. Our sun will then have run its course: "There shall be signs in the sun, and in the moon, and in the stars; and upon the earth distress of nations, with perplexity; the sea and the waves roaring" (Lk. 21:25). Our earth, according to the declarations of Scripture, will be destroyed by fire, as it was formerly by water, and will receive a more beautiful and spacious form. The dust will be animated with new life and glorified bodies adorned with celestial beauty will be prepared from it, for the souls of the redeemed. When the dead are raised, they will all recognize the Lord in His glory as their Judge, and they who on earth despised Him will then tremble and be dismayed and utter the wailings of despair. He will execute judgment on all with Divine omniscience, holiness, and rectitude and adjudge to each His final state, according to his righteousness or unrighteousness, whether to salvation or condemnation. Thus will He manifest Himself at the closing scene of the world's history as the Lord of lords and King of kings, as the Supreme Judge of the human race. But to us it is most consolatory to know that "the Father hath committed all judgment to the Son," and that, therefore, we shall be judged by One Who will sympathize with our infirmities, since He was tempted in all points as we are, but without sin. The judgment by which He will separate forever the good from the evil, and crush the power of sin, and death, and hell, will complete His state of exaltation and the revelation of His glory.

6

ON THE LOVE OF GOD

ON THE LOVE OF GOD AS THE SOURCE OF ALL HAPPINESS; AND ON SIN, WHICH DEPRIVES US OF HAPPINESS.

In our last Lecture we finished the consideration of the doctrine of Scripture respecting the Person of Christ. We now proceed to inquire what is taught in the Inspired Volume respecting the Work of Christ, or the purpose for which He became incarnate. The latter depends so entirely on the former, being as intimately connected with it as the branch with the stem, that in the representation we gave of the extraordinary constitution of Christ's person, we necessarily adverted to the object which it was designed to accomplish. If we attentively survey the delineation of the two natures of the Mediator, their union, and the various steps of His humiliation and exaltation and seriously consider the impression which the whole is fitted to make, we shall be convinced that the object and aim of His work is to effect a most intimate connection and communion between the Divinity and the human race, by which the love of God is to be gloriously displayed and the welfare and salvation of man established on an immoveable basis. The welfare of man as a rational, spiritual being is founded on the love of God and communion with Him. The highest, essential point of superiority in man above the irrational creation consists in this: *that he is capable of religion,* that he knows God and His Law, that he is created for the purpose of resembling and loving his Maker. In other properties the higher orders of animals, though not equal, are similar to man; the difference between them, though great, is only in degree. But of religion, as a self-conscious relation to God and the spiritual world, no trace can be found in the brute creation. Religion, the sacred band which unites man in spontaneous love to the Almighty Lord of the universe, makes man also the lord of the terrestrial creation. His physical strength, cunning, and prudence do not give him this pre-eminence, or if they do, it is at most only in reference to external objects; for supposing that he controls at his pleasure the inferior animals, his heart may all the while be enslaved by an attachment to some other created object, either to money and worldly possessions, or sensual indulgence, or splendor, or perhaps to one of his fellow-mortals. Faith and love alone set the heart free from bondage to the creature and enable man to control it instead of being controlled by it; they calm the soul, release it from the slavery of the passions, and elevate the whole man above the fettering influence of the changeable and perishable to the unchangeable and eternal. Religion, as the bond which connects man, the offspring of time, with the eternal, immortal God, is the basis of his immortality; which the temporal and changeable creature enjoys not as its own prerogative, but solely through its connection with the eternal and unchangeable. Religion is the proper destiny, the true happiness of man; it is the end of his creation; hence it is said, "Let us make man in Our Own likeness, and let them have dominion over all the earth" (Gen. 1:26). The image of God in man, or his likeness to God, is nothing else than religion—the connection or relationship of man with God—in consequence of which the light of Divine knowledge shines in his reason, his will acts in harmony with the Divine will, and his heart is governed by the affection of Divine love. To bear the image of God, by means of religion, was the destination of man, the design of his creation. Nor while this constitutes his supreme end is any useful mode of activity in concerns relating to the present world excluded—on the contrary: religion gives to all the diversified forms of human ability, which are, be it remembered, the gifts and endowments of the Creator, their genuine consecration, the purest motives, and the highest aim, and imparts to human agency a moral proportion, order, and harmony by which the Divine image is brought out in luster and beauty.

And as religion is the highest duty of man, so also it constitutes his happiness. The essence of happiness, as well as of religion, consists in the love of God; by which we mean, not merely our love to God, but more especially the love of God to us, and which we appropriate to ourselves by faith. God is in himself the highest perfection and happiness, the supreme good, and the source of all inferior good. Our highest good is when God is for us—that is, when He loves us. The love of God to us is not only in itself our highest happiness and enjoyment, but it is also the only fountain of all that is good and felicitous, of all that can afford content and satisfaction, either in this world or the next. It is not an inactive principle but is operating continually for our good; here on earth it bestows many precious gifts, and, if we continue in it, will bestow still greater and more magnificent gifts in heaven. But the love of God is of far greater value than the gifts it dispenses: it is the essence of our happiness, and without it all the riches of heaven would not make us happy, for we should still want the best, the highest good. For the same reason no accumulation of earthly good can make those persons happy who have not the love and peace of God, and to whom therefore real satisfaction is wanting.

The same principle holds good in mere human relations. It is love which imparts the greatest happiness in all the relations and connections of life. It is an inward affection of the heart not perceptible to the outward eye; not being an object of the senses, it must be enjoyed by faith. It is, however, not inoperative, but manifests itself outwardly and visibly by gifts and kind offices. These expressions of kindness are doubtless very gratifying, but what are they compared with the love of which they are the evidence? How would their value sink without it, and how much is their value enhanced by it! How much more precious is anything presented to us by love than the same thing purchased by money! And why? Because in the former case, in addition to the thing itself a far higher good is possessed, namely, the love of the giver. To value the gift more than the giver, to love any one not for himself and his love, but only for the sake of what he has and gives, betrays a mean and selfish spirit. But much more is this the case in reference to the Divine Being. God is to be loved most of all for what He is in Himself, and His love to us must be a far higher good than all His gifts and benefits. If love be the chief ingredient in happiness, and that, too, in proportion to the excellence of Him Whom we love, must not the love of the blessed and most high God make us most happy? His love is an ever-present, holy, pure, constant affection, which surrounds us entirely with its gentle but powerful influence, penetrates our inmost souls, takes cognizance of all our cares and anxieties, and sympathizes with all our joys and sufferings, even the most secret; an affection to which we can entrust our most hidden sorrows with the fullest confidence. On the bosom of such a love we repose so softly, in its arms we sleep so quietly, and find such consolation, peace, and security that he who enjoys these blessings is secure of everlasting bliss. And this eternal, highest good is continually imparting to us in greater or less abundance those benefits and gifts which naturally flow from it. For since the Divine love is full of vital energy, it dispenses good with an unsparing hand and bestows on us numberless invaluable benefits in childhood, in youth, and in old age, both for time and eternity. All that we are and have are its gifts; each additional day of our lives is an effect of its bounty.

Many, alas, are devoted entirely to their own selfish interests. They fondly cleave to the gift, but disregard the Giver. They enjoy their daily bread as the ox relishes its fodder, without a thought of the paternal goodness which provides it. They behold the sun rising in its splendor and rejoice in its light, but are never reminded of Him, Who at the creation said, and every morning repeats the command, "Let there be light." They see the beauty and utility of created things and employ them for their own use and pleasure, but without acknowledging the glory and excellency of Him Who created all things and "is the First Author of all beauty." They devote themselves with their whole heart to created things, which are passing away, and in their eager pursuit of honor, wealth, and pleasure, undergo the greatest drudgery. Yet they never attain the object of their wishes—real happiness, real inward joy, and repose—but are always striving, the more they have, to gain still more. They wear themselves out by anxiety, envy, and vexation, and at last leave at the edge of the grave all the trash they have spent their days in collecting, if it be not previously taken away from them. The human heart, which originally bore the impress of God's image, has within itself an ever-craving, infinite longing, which nothing can quiet or satisfy but God and His love. If a man possessed the whole world, he would not be long content but would soon sigh for another. But let him once obtain the love and peace of God, and his heart will enjoy repose and inward happiness; instead of coveting a world, a cottage will be enough for him. He will receive all the gifts and benefactions of the Divine love with an entirely different joy, far nobler than that of the unhappy mortal who has all things except God. He rejoices not only in the good things themselves which have fallen to his lot, but in that Divine love which has provided and bestowed them. They are all precious memorials to him of his beloved Lord and God; and though they are in their own nature transitory and perishable, or may be taken from him in the course of God's fatherly discipline, still there remains to him that eternal, unchanging, beatifying love, from which even tribulation and death cannot sever him, and which, after the trials of the present life are ended, shall enrich him with immortal blessings. Wherefore David says: "Thy loving-kindness is better than life" (Ps. 58:3); and the Apostle: "If God be for us, who can be against us?...In all these things we are more than conquerors through him that loved us" (Rom. 8: 31, 37); "and we know that all things work together for good to them that love God" (8:28). And, lastly, St. John, in his first epistle: "God is love, and he that dwelleth in love dwelleth in

God, and God in him" (1 Jn. 4:16).

Thus the love of God is the ground and essence of our happiness, and it is also the ground of our sanctification, without which there can be no real happiness, as the apostle declares, "Without holiness no man shall see the Lord" (Heb. 12:14). The most blessed effect of God's love to us, when received on our part with sincere faith, is our love to Him. Divine love so received necessarily produces in us a reciprocal love, and the goodness of God manifested in what He has done for us is a most powerful motive to our well-doing. "We love Him," saith St. John, "because He first loved us" (1 Jn. 4:19). Who can really believe the overflowing and wholly unmerited love of God towards us without being stimulated to a grateful filial love in return? Who would not be anxious to do the will of that Being Who has done and is doing so much for us? And such a love to God must be the only pure source of all that holy and virtuous conduct which is pleasing in His sight. "Love is the fulfilling of the law," saith St. Paul (Rom. 13:10). The first and great commandment of the Law is, "Thou shalt love the Lord thy God with all thy heart, and with all thy soul, and with all thy mind" (Matt. 22:37). Whoever fulfills this command, fulfills the whole law, for the love of God infallibly leads to the love of our neighbor and to a willing compliance with every intimation of the Divine will; it therefore as constantly and naturally produces good works as a good tree produces good fruit. But whoever does not fulfill this highest command, fulfills none, at least not in a manner pleasing to God, for that only can please God which is done from love to Him or is sanctified through that love. Even the love of our neighbor is only then of the right kind, when it is grounded on the love of God, because only on such a foundation can it be kept free from partiality and selfish views. Whatever in human conduct does not rest on this principle of Divine love, whatever is done from motives of self-interest—either to avoid punishment or gain a reward, even were it the punishment of hell and the reward of heaven, or to obtain honor and praise from the world, or to procure a return of good offices—may indeed appear praiseworthy and lovely in the eyes of men, who can judge only of the exterior; but in the sight of God, Who looks into the heart, it cannot be regarded as real holiness, nor can it gain His approbation and the happiness that flows from it.

It is therefore certain that we can be truly happy only through God's love to us, and truly good or righteous through our love to God. Thus it was with our first parents. God loved them when they were created in His image, and they loved God: in this reciprocal love they were good and happy, and enjoyed themselves in the innocence of paradise. But what is the fact respecting their descendants? respecting ourselves? Does God love us, and do we love God?

Can He love us, and can we love Him? Are we happy and holy? And if we are not, how can we become so? These are serious questions, which involve the most momentous consequences.

There is in truth a mighty and apparently insurmountable barrier raised against the exercise of love between God and man: this is sin, or moral evil. Sin is everything which is contrary to God's Law, whether a disposition of mind, the actual commission of evil, or the omission of duty. It could not exist at the creation of man, for God would never have created and established anything contrary to his own Law. Sin could enter into this our world, over which it has spread universally, only by man's own fault; for, as the Apostle declares, "All have sinned, and come short of the glory of God" (Rom. 3:23). There is no man who can stand before the Law of God as righteous and pure. The Scriptures inform us of the primary act of sin committed by our first parents, which was the original cause of all that followed and in its destructive consequences has propagated itself to all men, so that in reference to its effects it may be called the original sin. Without examining on this occasion more closely the origin and propagation of sin, we wish to consider sin as it actually exists in ourselves. It is not difficult to come to a just conclusion on this point, for in the Law of God we have an infallible rule of moral judgment. This Law accuses all men of a violation of its commands, and it will be no easy matter to repel this accusation; for everyone must confess that he has either done what was wrong or failed to do what was right. In proof of this I need only appeal to that monitor whose voice in softer or louder tones makes itself heard in the breast of every man. But man, prejudiced in his own favor, seeks to silence or to get rid of its accusations instead of fairly confronting them. He places by their side various good deeds, which, notwithstanding his occasional failings and infirmities, he ventures to flatter himself that he may boast of. Because in their dealings with their fellow-mortals men are obliged to make mutual allowances and concessions, and to set good qualities against bad ones, they think God will judge concerning them in like manner; and hence without making themselves very uneasy about their sins, they presume that their good deeds and partial obedience will counterbalance their offenses and transgressions. But this is a great and dangerous delusion. The judgment of the omniscient and all-holy God on our sins is declared in His Law, of which, since it is eternal truth and rectitude, not one tittle can fail. Every sin against the eternal command is eternal guilt, which cannot be obliterated by any subsequent performances of duty. If I fulfill my obligations to-day, that does not acquit me before the judgment-seat of the Divine rectitude for not fulfilling them yesterday, just as human law will not remit its claims on an individual, relative to his past conduct, merely because its present requirements are complied with. And even allowing that the Divine Law could relinquish its eternal claims upon our obedience for the past under the condition that for the future it should be fulfilled, the question arises: will it be really fulfilled? And can it at any time be completely satisfied? The answer must be, "No; it will never be fulfilled by us." Our outward conduct in deed—the works of our hands, our doing or leaving undone certain actions—may be so regulated in the sight of our fellow-creatures after former failings and delinquencies that neither the law of the state nor public opinion can detect any thing reprehensible. But can we with equal confidence subject our conduct to the Divine scrutiny? God looks not at the hand but at the heart, and what does He seek for there? For nothing less than what is required by the first great commandment of the Law—"Thou shalt love the Lord with all thy heart, with all thy soul, and with all thy mind." And what does God condemn in our hearts? All evil, selfish desires; for it stands written: "Thou shalt not covet." But what will God find in our hearts if he searches their inmost recesses with His all-penetrating eye? Will He ever find there that entirely sincere, cordial, self-renouncing love of His holy Law, whence alone can proceed filial and willing obedience to His commands? Will He not rather find there that we love ourselves most of all; that our principal and constant striving is after that which is agreeable, honorable, and advantageous to ourselves; that by nature we strive after that which pleases ourselves, rather than after that which pleases Him? And beholding such a disposition in our hearts, what value can our outward propriety of conduct have in His eyes? But if such be our real character, how can He love us, *and how can we be saved?*

7

THE LAW AND THE GOSPEL

ON THE DIFFERENCE BETWEEN THE LAW AND THE GOSPEL, AND THE IMPOSSIBILITY OF OBTAINING SALVATION BY THE FORMER.

A*nd how can we be saved?* With this question I closed the last lecture, and with the same question I begin this. It is of all questions the most important which a man can ask himself. May we lay it deeply to heart! The answer appears easy, and yet it is so difficult that no man by his unassisted reason can give it: it is to be found only in the Gospel of Jesus Christ. It is perfectly clear and certain that we attain goodness and happiness only through the love of God, and yet we can by nature derive no certainty of salvation from that source, for it is equally certain that without the love of God we can attain neither goodness nor happiness. But sin, as the opposite of goodness, operates as a complete obstacle to God's love towards us, as well as to our love towards God. If the love of God be our highest virtue and happiness, it is evident that the want of love to God must be our greatest vice and unhappiness. We have the united testimony of conscience and of the Divine Law that we are in a state of unrighteousness and unhappiness, totally different from that in which man was originally created. If we direct our serious attention to what passes within our own breasts, unless we willingly deceive ourselves, we shall find an accuser there who plainly tells us, "Thou art not worthy of God's love; thou art not worthy to be called His child; far from rendering Him that grateful love to which He is so justly entitled, thou hast abused His goodness and His favors; thou hast transgressed His holy Law." And when this accuser lifts up his voice against us, he will not allow himself to be silenced again—on the contrary: he will speak in louder and more threatening accents; nor shall we be able to conciliate him, for his appeal is to the Law of God. Now the Law, while it distinctly assures those who keep it that they shall enjoy God's love and eternal life, no less plainly threatens those who violate it with the wrath of God and eternal condemnation, as it is written: "Cursed be he that confirmeth not all the words of this Law to do them" (Deut. 27:26); and again: "Indignation and wrath, tribulation and anguish, upon every soul of man that doeth evil" (Rom. 2:8, 9). As the Divine love is zealous on behalf of all good, so the Divine holiness is zealous against all evil, for our God is a mighty and a jealous God. And since we are sinners in His sight, since we have not fulfilled the greatest commandment of the law, that of love, what can we expect from our righteous Judge, but to be cast away from His presence? Sin has broken the holy bond of love that once united man to his Creator, and we no longer view Him as a gracious Father, but as the righteous Judge, Who must pronounce sentence according to the Law. Either the Law of God is falsehood, or if it be truth, eternal truth (and it can be nothing else), then we stand as undone transgressors before the judgment-seat and can only in deep contrition sue for mercy and compassion. Many persons attempt to mitigate the severity of this sentence, but all in vain; they appeal to the Divine love, as if that could not be so strict; but they forget that the greatness of this love only enhances our guilt, for the more God has loved us, the greater the benefits He has conferred upon us, so much more heinous is the guilt of our ingratitude. The manifold proofs of the Divine benevolence furnished by our own personal experience and those which are manifested in nature around us can yield no consolation or relief when we think of the Divine rectitude, but rather appear as fresh accusers against us. Besides, the love of God cannot set aside his holiness, but must, on the contrary, support its claims in all their unqualified strictness.

Yet many imagine that God must needs vouchsafe His saving mercy and love to a sinner on his amendment. I reply, first, that it is incompatible with the essential strictness of the Law that the righteousness of the present time should expiate for the unrighteousness of the past; and, secondly, I deny that man in a state of sin can himself acquire a new righteousness, or by his own power can so far alter or amend himself as to regain the favor of God and become worthy of His love by any works of righteousness which he has done. The reason is obvious: nothing is of any value in the sight of God which does not proceed from sincere love to Him. Love to Him, which is the fulfillment of the first and great command, must be at the beginning and lie at the foundation of all genuine conversion or amendment. But how is it possible for man to possess this love, so long as in the consciousness of guilt he must dread God as his Judge? If he feel himself condemned and disowned by his Maker, how can he love Him? Or, rather, must he not shrink from His presence with dismay and terror? Under such circumstances he can render only the obedience of a slave, which, being destitute of filial love, cannot possibly be acceptable to God. The sinfulness of man is principally shown in his forsaking God and in seeking the gratification of self. To this the Scriptures refer, when it is said, "the imagination of man's heart is evil from his youth" (Gen. 8:21); this forms the essence of sin and our original depravity. For as the essence of righteousness or virtue is the love of God, so the essence of unrighteousness or sin is the love of self, which, since the Fall, has been the ruling principle in human nature and is continually producing in us a self-will that strives against the Divine will. As a corrupt tree cannot bring forth good fruit, so neither can this sinful disposition change itself into its opposite, which would be an absolute contradiction. Our natural free-will cannot effect such a change, for it is itself depraved by sin and would require a previous renovation. It has not the power by its dictates to produce or to destroy feelings or sentiments which exist in the heart. Love especially, if it be wanting, cannot be produced by an act of the will, and yet this affection towards God is our first duty, the obligation of which is in no degree lessened by our inability to fulfill it, for this very inability is a consequence and a part of our sin. St. Paul declares, "The carnal mind is enmity against God: for it is not subject to the Law of God, neither indeed can be; so then they that are in the flesh cannot please God" (Rom. 8:7, 8).

Thus it appears that, on account of the sinfulness and impurity of our hearts, not only have we no righteousness which can stand the scrutiny of a holy God, but we are unable by our own power to acquire such a righteousness. We are under the curse of the Law and are unable to redeem ourselves from it, nor is it in the power of any human or created being to redeem us, as it is written in Ps. 49:7: "None of them can by any means redeem his brother, nor give to God a ransom for him"; and Rom. 3:19: "Every mouth must be stopped, and all the world become guilty before God. Therefore by the deeds of the Law there shall no flesh be justified in His sight; for by the Law is the knowledge of sin." The Law, or the rule of moral conduct, instructs us in the knowledge of what is good or evil, righteous or unrighteous, but it gives us no power to become righteous: it gives us no disposition to live unto righteousness and to die unto sin, as the Apostle says: "If there had been a Law given which could have given life, verily righteousness should have been by the Law" (Gal. 3:21). But it can no more "give life" than a knowledge of his disease and danger can give health to a sick man. Of what use is it then to be enforcing moral obligations on men in whom the desire to fulfill them and the love of goodness are wanting? It will be of as much use as for a physician to be always telling his patients that they need restoration to health without attempting to apply a remedy. Of what use is it to promise men salvation, if they will only fulfill God's commands, when they do not fulfill them? It is as if a physician should promise his patients good health as soon as they should get rid of their pains and yet render them no assistance for that purpose. The Law is a good and correct direction-post to heaven, but of what use is the direction-post with its wooden arm as long as the power of walking is wanting? Can the direction-post raise and carry the traveller, and bring him to his journey's end? So far from the Law being able to lead man to the first end and aim of his creation—to righteousness and happiness—it will, on the contrary, if help and salvation do not arise from some other quarter, only aggravate the misery of his condition: "The Law worketh wrath," saith the Apostle (Rom. 4:15). The knowledge of the greatness of our ruin and of the necessity of redemption, connected with our inability to effect it, will only aggravate and embitter the unhappiness of our condition, place us at a greater distance from God, and plunge us at last after fruitless attempts at repentance either into despair, or, it may be (which is quite as bad), into a cold indifference and hardened presumption. Indeed, for we find that all men who have not embraced the Gospel live either in a state of thoughtless security and utter contempt of the first injunctions of the Divine Law, or in one of painful disquietude and self-tormenting fear, in attempting to establish a righteousness of their own, which in the sight of God will be null and void. This deadly effect of the Law is not to be imputed to itself, but to our guilt: it is the consequence of our sin, as St. Paul says: "The Law is holy, and the commandment holy, and just, and good. But sin, that it might appear sin, worketh death in me by that which is good; that sin by the commandment might become exceeding sinful" (Rom. 7:12, 13). Hence, the Apostle at the close of his argument respecting the Law was obliged to say, and we too must join in the confession, "O wretched man that I am, who shall deliver me from the body of this death?" But after this expression of anguish and contrition, he joyfully adds, "I thank God through Jesus Christ our Lord" (Rom. 7:24, 25).

The Gospel of Jesus Christ alone leads us to happiness and salvation, as the Apostle declares: "What the Law could not do, in that it was weak through the flesh, God did, sending His own Son in the likeness of sinful flesh, and for sin condemned sin in the flesh" (Rom. 8:3). God has effected through His mercy that which was impossible to sinful man through the Law. It must ever be impossible for man to be justified and saved by the Law, for it accuses him as an evil-doer and pronounces him reprobate; while, weakened as he is by sin, he cannot satisfy its demands. That intercourse of love between God and man wherein our happiness consists, having been interrupted by sin, cannot be renewed on our part. Once separated from God, we cannot by our own power return to him any more than one who has fallen into deep water can pull himself out by his own arm. We should therefore remain forever separated from God by sin and be given up to condemnation, if He did not of His own free grace draw nigh to us; if He did not put forth the raising and helping hand of reconciliation; if He did not on His part unite again the torn band of love, and for Christ's sake forgive our sins. Let us suppose the case of two persons, a superior and an inferior. The latter has repaid all the kindness and good offices of the former with ingratitude and disobedience, but at last finds himself deprived of the kindness and aid of his benefactor, exposed to misery, and visited with condign punishment. He would gladly be reconciled to his superior, but how can this be accomplished? The gifts and benefits which he has received have been squandered away; his precious time has been misspent; nothing has been done which ought to have been done. How shall he escape his anger? By what means shall he regain his lost love? By the penitent emotions of his heart? Impossible! For as long as he is not assured of the favor of his offended lord, his only feelings must be those of dread and remorse, which can only prompt to slavish acts of fear and constraint. Thus the prodigal son, before his father had received him with open arms, did not venture to promise himself more than to be as one of his hired servants (Lk. 15:19). But could the performance of a hired servant's work make him worthy of his father's love? Evidently not. How, then, could the former relation of love be re-established? Only in this way—by the father's forgiving the son, not on account of his own worthiness (for that did not exist,) but of his own free compassion, coming forward to meet him with undeserved kindness and gratuitously bestowing upon him his forfeited love. Thus we read in the parable: "And when he was yet a great way off, his father saw him and had compassion and ran and fell on his neck and kissed him." With such unmerited love does our heavenly Lord and Father come forward to meet the sinner, comforts his heart torn with anguish, restores to him peace and rest, imparts to him the Spirit of adoption, and awakens in his bosom a grateful, filial love, which manifests itself in new obedience and in works well-pleasing to God, whereas before he could render only the service of a hireling. We see then that reconciliation and redemption must originate not from earth, but from heaven; not from sinful man, but from God against Whom he has sinned.

Such is the relation between God and man in the Gospel. The Gospel in the strict sense of the term is the joyful annunciation of the free mercy of God in Christ Jesus, bestowed upon sinners without any merit or desert of their own. It is essentially distinguished from the Law and indeed in many points stands in direct contrast to it. The consideration of this difference is of the greatest importance, in order to our reception of the saving truths of Christianity. The Law is an uncompromising assertion of the Divine holiness; it commands man to love God with all his heart and to hold all His precepts sacred. The Gospel is the gracious announcement of the Divine mercy, which assures man of God's love towards him and His readiness to forgive him all his sins. The Law demands love from man; the Gospel bestows love upon man. The Law teaches man what ought to be his conduct towards God; the Gospel informs him what has been God's conduct towards man. The Law requires an offering from man; the Gospel brings gifts to man. The Law demands; the Gospel bestows. The Law ordains; the Gospel promises. The Law charges us with sin; the Gospel pardons it. The Law denies salvation to the sinner; the Gospel grants it. The Law accuses and condemns; the Gospel justifies and accepts us. The Law pronounces a curse upon us; the Gospel changes the curse into everlasting blessings.

It may, indeed, be said, that the Law has also its promises, as, for instance: "This do, and thou shalt live" (Lk. 10:28); "The doers of the Law shall be justified" (Rom. 2:13); but these promises are attached to a previous fulfillment of its commands. Now, no man has fulfilled, but every man has violated them so that no one can appropriate to himself the promise any more than a person can appropriate to his own use an article of merchandise for which he has not paid down the equivalent price. The declaration is true that "the doers of the Law shall be justified," but it is equally true that those who are *not* doers of the Law (and such are all men, for all are sinners) shall not be justified, and consequently cannot apply to themselves the promises, but only the threatenings of the Law. The promises of the Gospel, on the other hand, are free and not restricted by our previous worthiness; they are not grounded on our virtue or our merit, but only on the greatness and depth of the Divine love, which, self-moved, and out of pure grace, has had compassion on our fallen race, as a mother has compassion on her little one, though it be sick and feeble, unclean and deformed. Hence the Gospel appears with the most inviting aspect in the Holy Scriptures: its very name, which means "glad tidings," is full of kindness. Under the Jewish economy, Elijah witnessed a symbolical representation of it, when, "after the great and strong wind, which brake the rocks in pieces," "the earthquake," and "the fire," (fit emblems of the Law!) "a still small voice passed by," betokening the presence of Jehovah. It is the gentle crook of the good Shepherd, Who collects His wandering and drooping sheep, leads them by "the green pastures and the still waters," and carries the weary and sick in His arms (Isa. 40:11). The great Messenger and Surety of the Gospel is called "the Lamb of God, Which takes away the sin of the world." He is described as the Bridegroom "Who loved the church, and gave Himself for it"; as a King Who is meek and lowly in heart, Who gives rest to the weary and heavy laden, Whose yoke is easy, and Whose burden is light, of Whom also it is said: "How beautiful upon the mountains are the feet of Him that bringeth good tidings of good, that publisheth salvation; that saith unto Zion, 'Thy God reigneth.'" In short, the most gentle, lovely, and inviting images are employed in Scripture in order to impress upon us the infinite grace and kindness of the Gospel and its Author in contrast to the Law, which is represented as the awful voice of God, as a consuming fire, as the sound of mighty thunderings, at which all nature trembles, as a hammer breaking the rock in pieces, as a two-edged sword, dividing asunder the joints and marrow.

However distinct and even opposite the two parts of Divine revelation, the Law and the Gospel, may be, yet a real harmony exists between them, and both unitedly contribute to our salvation. It is a very partial and unworthy representation of the Divine Being to speak of God as mere love and goodness and to represent Him as destitute of everything inflexibly just, awful, and majestic. The Lord is indeed mild and reviving as a gentle evening breeze, but He is also mighty as a whirlwind, fearful as an earthquake, consuming as a fire. Thus it is written: "The Lord thy God is a consuming fire, even a jealous God" (Deut. 4:24); and of the same God Who declared Himself to be "merciful and gracious, long-suffering, and abundant in goodness and truth, keeping mercy for thousands, forgiving iniquity and transgression and sin"—of Him also it is said, "If I whet My glittering sword, and Mine hand take hold on judgment, I will render vengeance to mine enemies and will reward them that hate Me. A fire is kindled in My anger and shall burn unto the lowest hell" (Deut. 32:22, 41). Thus Christ is styled "the Lamb of God" and "the Lion of the tribe of Judah." In that partial and inaccurate representation of the Divine character to which we have referred, which attributes to it nothing more than easy good nature, not only all the living energy of justice and rectitude disappears, but even the love of God loses all its power and worth. As in the Divine Being holiness and love, justice and mercy, are most intimately united, so also the manifestation of these two classes of attributes is harmoniously displayed in the method of human salvation. The Law, indeed, can never justify and save, but it leads man to the source of salvation and happiness. Our Lord says: "They that be whole need not a physician, but they that are sick: I am not come to call the righteous, but sinners to repentance" (Matt. 9:12, 13). And on another occasion, He declared: "The Son of man is come to seek and to save that which was lost"; and, "The Spirit of the Lord hath anointed Me to preach the Gospel to the poor; He hath sent me to heal the broken-hearted, to preach deliverance to the captives" (Luk. 4:18). What is a physician to those who consider themselves in health? What is a deliverer to those who do not consider themselves ruined?

Of what use is food to him whose hunger is satiated, or drink to him who is not thirsty, or gifts to him who esteems himself rich? How should he apply to be healed, who feels not the smart of his wounds? And how should he sigh for liberty, who is unconscious of his bondage? In order that Christ should be received by us, that He should become our Redeemer and Savior, we must first be sensible that we are weak and poor, in captivity and in bondage, lost and ruined. But this state of mind is produced by the Law, for by it we obtain the true knowledge of sin. By its stern denunciations it destroys all self-conceit and self-dependence, and shows us, as in a clear mirror, that our own righteousness is in the sight of God no better than a polluted garment; it lays open our most secret faults and makes us sensible of the danger and virulence of that disease which none but a heavenly Physician can cure; it discovers our inward poverty and nakedness and smites us with the rod of correction, till in the anguish of our souls we cry out, "God be merciful to me a sinner!" But the mighty wind, the earthquake, and the fire, are followed by the gentle sounds of the gospel, and the mild benignant voice of the good Shepherd is heard, saying, "Son, be of good cheer; thy sins be forgiven thee!" (Matt. 9:2). And the heart is revived by those gracious words: "Blessed are the poor in spirit, for theirs is the kingdom of heaven. Blessed are they that mourn, for they shall be comforted. Blessed are they which do hunger and thirst after righteousness, for they shall be filled." When the heart believes this with confidence, it is filled with that holy joy of which the Apostle writes: "Therefore being justified by faith, we have peace with God through our Lord Jesus Christ, by Whom also we have access by faith into this grace wherein we stand, and rejoice in hope of the glory of God. And hope maketh not ashamed; because the love of God is shed abroad in our hearts by the Holy Ghost which is given unto us" (Rom. 5:1, 2, 5).

8

ON THE SATISFACTION OF CHRIST

IT was shown in the last Lecture that sinful man cannot be justified and saved by his own attempts to satisfy the requirements of the Law, but that he must be indebted to the grace of God, as manifested in the Gospel, which by a method entirely free forgives his sins and unrighteousness and makes him again a partaker of the Divine favor. Before proceeding farther, it will be best to dispose of a question which may possibly disturb and perplex many minds. It is this: if men can be saved only by the grace of the Gospel, what will become of the poor heathen who have not known it and could not know it, since it was never published to them? I answer that it would be manifestly absurd to suppose that that can be true of heathens which is denied concerning Christians: that they can be saved by their own merits. No; if Christians have no merit of their own before God, certainly those who are not Christians can have none. If the works of Christians, even such as in the eyes of their fellow-creatures appear most excellent and lovely, are not free in the sight of God from a greater or less alloy of self, the good works of heathens performed without the influence of grace must be far less pure, although in relation to the present world we readily allow their value and good repute. But in the sight of God there is no difference: "all have sinned and come short of His glory." Therefore on the ground of works and merit, no man—and consequently none of the heathen—can be saved. Yet it is written: "God will have all men to be saved, and to come unto the knowledge of the truth" (1 Tim. 2:4); "Jesus Christ is the propitiation for our sins: and not for ours only, but also for the sins of the whole world" (1 Jn. 2:2). We venture therefore to hope that the Divine grace has methods of communicating in due time and place its blessings to those from whom, without their fault, a knowledge of saving truth has been withheld. And yet we must maintain that although God "will have all men to be saved," He will effect this only by the knowledge of the truth and not by error and sin; and, therefore, though we would not despair of the salvation of any man, there can be only one true way of obtaining eternal happiness, which is pointed out by the Gospel of the grace of God. All other religions at the best only profess to be various modifications of the Law, which in no shape whatever can bring man to salvation and eternal life. They all represent the work of reconciliation as beginning with something on the part of man in order to render the Deity propitious, for they all prescribe certain good works and supposed meritorious acts, offerings, and ceremonies which yet cannot atone to the Most High for sin, remove its guilt, and satisfy the claims of His justice. The Gospel alone begins the work of reconciliation, sanctification, and salvation with what God does for man, with His grace anticipating our necessities, and informs us that since our offences against the Law are too great for man to expiate,

God has freely forgiven and acquitted him, as Paul says: "For by grace are ye saved through faith, and that not of yourselves; it is the gift of God; not of works, lest any man should boast" (Eph. 2:8); "Not by works of righteousness which we have done, but according to His mercy He saved us" (Titus 3:5); "Being justified freely by His grace, through the redemption that is in Christ Jesus" (Rom. 3:24).

But here an important question arises: can God, all at once, by a simple act of mercy remit the whole debt contracted by sinners against His Law, freely forgive all their offences, withdraw the threatenings of His holy wrath against evil, and without any merit on the part of the sinner bestow upon him the Divine love and place him again in a filial relation to Himself? Would He not, by so doing, contradict Himself, since He would in fact rescind His holy Law, withdraw His requirements, nullify His threatenings, and violate His truth? If God pardoned sin so easily and thus ceased to maintain the inviolability of His commands, should we not be led to imagine that in giving the Law He had never been in earnest, or at least had ceased to be so; or that He now relaxed His requirements, because they had been enforced heretofore with undue severity? But in this case what would become of His veracity and faithfulness? And still further, where would be the due regard for His holiness and its just wrath against sin? And where would be the authority of His law? Would not levity scatter it to the winds, licentiousness burst all its bands, and impiety tread it under foot? And all this would be done under the pretense of magnifying the Divine grace in freely forgiving all sin! Truly, if God treated the forgiveness of sin as that slight matter which some represent it to be, not only would He Himself dishonor His holy majesty, but this earth would soon become a hell, the distinction between good and evil would be obliterated, and the sanctity of the moral Law would be scorned and violated.

But it cannot be; it is absolutely impossible, that the All-Wise and Most Holy should act thus. The sins of men against God's righteous Law cannot be forgiven, the world cannot be reconciled to God, the happiness we have forfeited cannot be restored, unless such a satisfaction be made to the Law that even in the very act of pardoning sinners its holy authority may be firmly upheld, and, while all sin is forgiven, justice is maintained in all its honors. But in what can this satisfaction consist? Only in a perfect fulfillment of the Law; in perfect obedience to its commands during a whole life, and in the holy endurance of the punishment annexed to its violation, as it is said of our Lord: "He became obedient unto death, even the death of the cross." This is the only offering, the only sacrifice for sin, which truly pleases, fully satisfies, and perfectly reconciles the Deity, since it is truly, fully, and perfectly conformable to His holy will. He who presents such a perfect sacrifice to God doubtless must be righteous in His sight, worthy of His love, and deserving of eternal happiness. But where can such a being be found who is able to make a satisfaction which shall be sufficient for the sins of the whole world? Evidently there are only two modes of accomplishing this: either the world itself, the whole human race, must present it, or a Being of equal or superior worth to the whole world. And such is the Son of God in His assumed humanity. Men cannot make satisfaction for themselves; they cannot by their own merit reconcile themselves to God, for until their sins are forgiven, they are unable to love God as His children; they merely stand in awe of Him. As long as they do not feel a child-like love, they cannot render a sincere and perfect obedience to His Law, and therefore cannot by their works be reconciled to Him, or regain His love. But let it be supposed that God should create a pure and sinless man, like our first parent before the Fall, yet such a one could not with his perfect human righteousness satisfy the Law for another, since he would be under obligations to fulfill that righteousness on his own account; still less could the merit of one mere man counterbalance the demerit of all the rest. The case would be similar if an angel or ministering spirit from a higher world were willing to descend to our earth. Besides, it would be extremely severe, even in the case of a voluntary offering, arbitrarily to let an innocent creature suffer for the guilty, and on the part of God no evidence would be afforded of a special love towards man.

Since the world then could not offer that satisfaction, without which the forgiveness of sin is impossible, the ancient saying, *Fiat justitia et pereat mundus*—"Let justice have its course, even though the world should perish"—must have been fulfilled, and we must all have been lost forever, had not the holy compassion of God, according to His eternal counsel, most wonderfully united in Jesus Christ righteousness and peace, mercy and truth, and thus made the forgiveness of sin possible, without impairing in the least degree the authority of the Law. How this has been accomplished, we are taught by the Apostle: "God sent forth His Son, made of a woman, made under the Law, to redeem them that were under the Law, that we might receive the adoption of sons" (Gal.4:4). And again: "Christ hath redeemed us from the curse of the Law, being made a curse for us" (Gal. 3:13); "God was in Christ, reconciling the world unto Himself, not imputing their trespasses unto them; for He hath made Him to be sin for us Who knew no sin, that we might be made the righteousness of God in Him" (2 Co.

5:19-21). And Peter declares: "Who His own self bare our sins in His own body on the tree, that we, being dead to sin, should live unto righteousness" (1 Pet. 2:24). And Isaiah under the old dispensation clearly prophesied: "All we like sheep have gone astray; we have turned every one to his own way; and the Lord hath laid on Him the iniquity of us all. He was wounded for our transgressions, He was bruised for our iniquities: the chastisement of our peace was upon Him; and with His stripes we are healed." Thus also Christ Himself declared: "The Son of Man came to give His life a ransom for many."

The more closely we examine these weighty expressions, the more profound will be our sense of the depths of Divine compassion and of the strictness of the Divine holiness; we shall thus learn rightly to apprehend and properly to estimate the great design of the Incarnation and the inestimable blessings which it confers upon us. We are taught that the Son of God became man not merely to announce the mercy of God to our race through the Gospel—for this purpose a messenger of inferior dignity might have sufficed—but principally in order to satisfy the Divine Law in His life, sufferings, and death, to obtain forgiveness for all human sin and guilt, and then to restore the partakers of this grace to the love of God, and their filial relation to Him. The forgiveness of sin without complete satisfaction, would be incompatible with the perfect holiness of God, the dignity of His justice, and the truth of His law, and would tend rather to the destruction than the salvation of His creatures. A world of sinners could not by any efforts of their own render that satisfaction, and yet this was absolutely necessary for their restoration to happiness. What then was performed by the Divine compassion? "God so loved the world that He gave His only-begotten Son, that whosoever believeth on Him should not perish, but have everlasting life" (Jn. 3:16). The Son of God, Who was truly Lord and God, submitted according to His Father's will, and from the free impulse of His own love as man to the Law, and fulfilled it from His birth to His death, even the death of the cross, both actively and passively, living and dying, even as men must have fulfilled it in order to regain the Divine love, to be just in the sight of the Law, and to become worthy of eternal happiness. This is the great and more excellent sacrifice, which, being presented by the Eternal High Priest, has made reconciliation for the sins of the world, as it is written in the Epistle to the Hebrews: "Christ being come, an High Priest of good things to come, not by the blood of goats and calves, but by His own blood, He entered in once into the holy place, having obtained eternal redemption for us. For if the blood of bulls and of goats, and the ashes of an heifer sprinkling the unclean, sanctifieth to the purifying of the flesh, how much more shall the blood of Christ, Who through the Eternal Spirit offered Himself without spot to God, purge your conscience from dead works to serve the living God?" (Heb. 9:11-14). "This man, after He had offered one sacrifice for sins, forever sat down on the right hand of God" (10:12). This offering of eternal efficacy and infinite worth evidently as much exceeds the sin and guilt of mankind as God is greater than man. If men had been desirous of reconciling themselves to God and justifying themselves by His law, they must have yielded perfect obedience as the only offering which could be accepted, for obedience is the true sacrifice and reasonable service demanded by it (Rom. 12:1). But this they were unable to render, and, consequently, on the ground of the Law, must stand condemned. Then the Son laid aside the glory of His Godhead, more glorious than all earthly glory; descended to this world with a Divine love, far greater than all human love; denied Himself with a self-denial far more severe than any mere creature, however exalted, could practice; and in the deepest humility rendered an obedience to the Law, even to the death of the cross, which was as perfect as it was voluntary and Divine. This obedience He rendered not like the first man, amidst the pleasures of a paradisaical life, but involved in all those earthly woes which are the effect of sin, amidst persecution and scorn, suffering and sorrow, and a bitter death. The greater the contrast between this depth of humiliation and the height of the Divine glory, so much greater is the value of the sacrifice presented by the Son of God in His assumed humanity to the Law. How could the Deity more impressively and emphatically manifest to the world the inviolability of His holy Law, with all its precepts and penalties, than by submitting to it, fulfilling its commands, and suffering its penalties in the form of that race who had been placed under it and had transgressed it? And since such an obedience to the Law could not be obligatory on the Deity Himself, but He must have submitted to it by an act of voluntary condescension, how could His love and compassion, as well as His holiness, be more gloriously manifested than when we are assured that all this submission to the Law, both in doing and suffering, was for us and for our benefit, in order that without detriment to its authority we might be redeemed from the curse, obtain the forgiveness of sins, and receive the blessing of adoption into the family of God! And this declaration and promise, without which we could scarcely believe the possibility of such mercy, is presented so clearly and explicitly in the passages we have quoted that it is hardly needful to adduce others, for they express in the most definite terms the vicarious satisfaction of our Lord.

In the whole life of Jesus, from His childhood to His death on the cross, we behold an example of the highest and most perfect righteousness, and this righteousness displays at the same time the purest, most self-renouncing love, for it was performed not for His own sake, but for ours. Our childhood has been sanctified by His; our maturer age by His; our whole life and death by His. Without abrogating the Law, He redeemed us from its bondage, when He, as a most faithful and holy Surety, discharged all our debt. Without retracting a single letter of the Law, He fulfilled it most completely, in order that our transgression of it might be pardoned. Without calling in question the justice of its curse, He bore and endured it as a lamb, in order that we might attain peace and happiness. He died the death of the cross in order to gain for us everlasting life. "He Who knew no sin," says the Apostle, "was made sin for us"—that is, was treated as a sinner—"that we might be made the righteousness of God in Him" that we might be treated as just in God's sight. He took our place, and we were allowed to occupy His; our sin became His sin, and His righteousness became our righteousness; our debt became His debt, and His merit became our merit; His poverty became our riches, as it is written: "Though He was rich, yet for your sakes He became poor, that ye through His poverty might become rich" (2 Cor. 8:9). "The Lord hath laid on Him the iniquity of us all," says Isaiah; "the chastisement of our peace was upon Him." His wounds are our healing; His death is our life; His sorrows are the source of our consolation; His sufferings are the ground of our happiness; His cross is the instrument of our glorification. And let us continually bear in mind Who it was that made this wonderful exchange of humiliation and suffering for our salvation: it was God, the Lord Himself. The Father gave the eternal Son; and the Son gave Himself for us, and in our nature manifested all the severity and all the goodness of God, receiving in His own person all the rigor of the Law and bestowing on us all the clemency of the Gospel.

This subject presents a contrast the greatness, depth, and fullness of which no language can express. Who can worthily praise love so infinite, so holy? Or rather, who can form any adequate conception of it? How great, how immeasurable is the love of our Lord! How tender is His compassion! How beneficent is His goodness! And yet at the same time how awful is His holiness! If we consider this latter attribute alone, there appears no grace, no compassion, no mercy—nought but the infliction of punishment. But by whom was the inexorable severity of God's Law endured? By Himself—by Him Who as man stood in the place of sinners, Who was made a curse for us that we might inherit the blessing, Who for our sakes "took upon Himself the form of a servant"..."that we might receive the adoption of sons." Ever cherish in your hearts the remembrance of this deep, holy, self-denying love. Let your inmost souls be moved by its mighty power; surrender yourselves without reserve to its attraction, and then decide whether they are in the right who say that the doctrine of Christ's satisfaction and of salvation by grace tends to make men think lightly of sin, or to foster sloth and negligence in the performance of good works, under the notion that Christ has done enough, and that the Law has been fulfilled and sin atoned for.

It has also been objected that the doctrine of Christ's satisfaction represents God as intolerably harsh and severe, since He would not forgive without a bloody satisfaction. But this allegation may be changed into an argument in its favor if we only maintain (what is not maintained by its opponents) the true

Divinity of Christ, on which the doctrine of His satisfaction is founded, for then the severity and rigor complained of affects not the guilty, nor a third guiltless party, but the Lord and Judge Himself, Who endured it all that we might be exempt from punishment. In proportion to the sacrifices He made and the sufferings He endured on our account must be the greatness and intensity of His love, as he who has rushed into the flames in order to rescue me gives a far stronger proof of affection than a person who only stands at a distance and points out how I may save myself or sends another to assist me. This view is supported by a passage of Scripture, already quoted, "The Church of God, which He hath purchased with His own blood." The severity, therefore, which is attributed to the doctrine of propitiation is exactly that feature of it which manifests the exceeding strength of God's holy love, for by the severity of the sufferings of Christ we may estimate the greatness of the Divine compassion. The distinction between the Father and the Son does not affect the justness of this representation; for we are not to consider the Son as all love, and the Father as all severity—both these qualities are in each of the sacred persons. The Father loves the Son, "His express image," as Himself, infinitely more than any earthly father can love an earthly son, and exhibits at the same time as convincing an evidence of His mingled love and severity in not withholding His Son as the Son Himself does in giving Himself up for our sakes. The primary ground of reconciliation is the love of God, but this can be manifested towards sinners only in constant union with the strictest holiness. That this is the doctrine of Scripture appears from St. John's Gospel: "God so loved the world, that He gave His only-begotten Son" (Jn. 3:16); and from the language of St. Paul: "God commendeth His love towards us, in that while we were yet sinners, Christ died for us" (Rom. 5:8).

With respect to the objection that the doctrine under consideration is of injurious moral tendency, it would be in vain to argue this question with a man who through unbelief is a stranger to its sanctifying power. Such a person, having no perception of the real power of love in the human breast, cannot conceive of the possibility of being governed or urged to obey God's commands unless by the scourge of the Law, by the dread of punishment, or by the prospect of gain; to act simply from love or gratitude seems to him utterly impracticable. But are threatenings of punishment and promises of reward the only or the worthiest means of engaging or impelling men to goodness? Is it not a slavish, selfish, and merely external obedience which proceeds from such motives? Is it not far nobler, more touching, and more powerful, to excite men by love to a love in return, to engage them by the attraction of goodness to a course of right action, to lay them under obligations by benefits, and that thus men should be led to disinterested well-doing? Thus an entire surrender of the heart will be made, and thus a cheerful, hearty obedience, which alone has any moral worth, will be produced. How indeed is it possible that any one possessing the heart of a man can believe in the infinite love and compassion of God in Christ Jesus, Who gave Himself on the cross for our sins, without being impelled to a thankful cordial love for such goodness and beneficence; without surrendering himself to his Redeemer in return for His condescension, and striving with his whole soul to obey and please Him? Such a man will act not as if wishing to gain something for himself, or to obtain a special reward, for the highest good, the love of God, has already been freely bestowed upon him. No, but he will act because under the influence of love he is neither able nor willing to do otherwise, and is desirous of showing (to use the expression of Novalis) that "gratitude has not yet become extinct on earth." Is it possible that anyone could despise, or grieve, or injure the friend who had saved his life at the hazard of his own? Would he not, on the contrary, gladly embrace every opportunity of pleasing and serving him and if possible make him a similar return of kindness? In like manner, it is impossible that the holy doctrine of redemption by the sufferings and death of Christ should ever make anyone who believes it from the heart careless or slothful, or indifferent to goodness. The contemplation of the Redeemer's cross must in every believer call forth the deepest emotions both of sorrow and joy and produce a renovation of the heart and life. He can no longer live unto sin, for which his Lord died, as St. Peter declares: "Who His own self bare our sins in His own body on the tree, that we, being dead to sins, should live unto righteousness" (Pet. 2:24). He cannot by willful disobedience slight and grieve the Friend Who obtained life for him by His own death, for this would be to aggravate the guilt of every other sin by ingratitude. Constrained by the love of Christ, he must consecrate his whole heart and life to His service and strive by progressive sanctification to become more intimately united to Him. It is only from such sentiments as these that genuine filial obedience and the new righteousness that is pleasing to God can arise, whilst all who continue under the Law and reject the Gospel are only as hirelings before God, and as they are, such will be their reward.

9

ON THE METHOD OF SALVATION

THE Word of God and the Sacraments are the divinely appointed means of grace, whereby, under the guiding influence of the Holy Spirit, we are led to salvation in Christ. But the Spirit of God, Who has all things under His control, makes use of many other preparatives or indirect means for leading men to salvation: such are the voice of reason and conscience, the sufferings and trials of life, and extraordinary events in the course of Providence. But these manifold admonitions and remonstrances are in vain if they do not bring us to the only source and fountain of eternal life. They may indeed excite the thirst, but they cannot quench it; they may make us sensible of our disease and our need of a physician, but they cannot effect a cure: this can be produced only by the Spirit of God, through the means of grace, Whose agency these indirect means may subserve, but without Whom they can accomplish nothing. Let us now consider the gracious operations of the Holy Spirit, whereby men are brought to salvation, in their orderly succession. Combined together they constitute the method of salvation and may be distinguished into five steps.

The first step is *calling,* or the Divine invitation and excitement to seek salvation. This takes place indirectly by all the warnings of God, in our own hearts and in the world around us, which tell us that salvation is not to be found in nature and direct us to a higher source. It is also done still more powerfully by the Law of God. But the direct instrument for this purpose is the Gospel, which contains an invitation from the God of heaven for all men to lay hold by faith on the offered salvation in Christ and to enter into His kingdom of grace: "Repent, and believe the Gospel—the kingdom of God is at hand" (Mk. 1:15). With this proclamation our Lord began His own public ministry, and the same is still addressed by His servants to men of every description. In Matthew 9:13 He says, "I am not come to call the righteous, but sinners to repentance." "Come unto Me, all ye that labor and are heavy-laden, and I will give you rest. Take My yoke upon you and learn of me; for I am meek and lowly in heart, and ye shall find rest unto your souls" (Matt. 11:28, 29). Hence also the Gospel is compared to a feast to which the Lord invites men by His servants and messengers, saying, "Come, for all things are ready" (Lk. 14:17). The first messengers were the apostles, and after them all the preachers of the true gospel, as St. Paul says: "We are ambassadors for Christ, as though God did beseech you by us; we pray you in Christ's stead, be ye reconciled unto God" (2 Cor. 5:20). Thus also the same apostle exclaims: "Awake thou that sleepest, and arise from the dead, and Christ shall give thee light" (Eph. 5:14). Similar language is used under the Old Testament dispensation by the prophet Isaiah: "Arise, shine; for thy light is come, and the glory of the Lord is risen upon thee" (Isa. 50:1). Thus the voice of God addresses us continually in the Divine Word and finds an echo in our breasts which repeats the call: "Awake thou that sleepest, prepare to meet thy God." Thus it is true at all times that "many are called, but few are chosen," since so many turn a deaf ear to the warning voice and are seduced by the allurements of the flesh and of the world (Matt. 20:16).

Secondly to calling succeeds *Divine illumination.* "Arise, shine," says the voice of God, "for thy light is come. Arise from the dead, and Christ shall give thee light." Divine revelation is represented throughout the Bible as the great source of illumination to mankind respecting their highest and everlasting good so that those persons who are not willing implicitly to rely on this revelation show themselves to be—according to the Scriptures—blind leaders of the blind and lovers of darkness rather than light (Jn. 3:19). Christ especially is called the True Light of the world (Jn. 1:9), and He says of Himself: "I am the Light of the world; he that followeth Me shall not walk in darkness, but shall have the light of life" (Jn. 8:12). Without Him we walk in darkness, not knowing either God or ourselves aright. But if we obey his heavenly call then the Holy Spirit enlightens us by the Word and not only communicates through the Law a conviction of our sinfulness and need of redemption, but also through the Gospel a knowledge of the redeeming mercy of God in Christ. For "God hath shined into our hearts to give the light of the knowledge of the glory of God in the face of Jesus Christ" (2 Cor. 4:6). The dismal night of doubt and fear, of ignorance respecting God and our real welfare, is dispersed, the day of light and love breaks in upon us (Rom. 13:12), and the "eyes of our understanding are enlightened, that we may know what is the hope of His calling, and what the riches of the glory of His inheritance" (Eph. 1:18).

In the third and fourth place illumination is followed by

repentance and *faith,* which joined together constitute true conversion, or the renovation and moral transformation of man. Repentance or contrition is at first effected by means of the Law, which convinces men of the impurity of their nature, the enormity of sin, and their inability to redeem themselves, and thereby fills them with grief and anguish before God. This condition is rendered more painful in proportion as the Law, with its pure and holy light, illuminates the whole man and penetrates more deeply into the recesses of his heart. There it discovers—perhaps under the fair veil of a life moral and honorable before the world—such a want of heartfelt love and devotedness to God, such coldness and ingratitude; so much selfishness, and such an absence of self-denial; so much restlessness and passion, and such a want of quietness and patience; so much levity and dissipation, and so little seriousness and self-possession; so much irritability and rashness, and so little gentleness and forbearance to others; so much bitterness against our enemies, and so little pity for them; so much anxiety to please men, and so little to please God; so much fondness for talking, and so little for prayer; so many good resolutions, and so unfrequent a fulfillment of them; and, above all, so many impure wishes and inclinations, that the man dare not raise his eyes to meet the eyes of his Maker, which are as a flame of fire, but must confess that he is indeed a poor sinner. Yes, we must acknowledge with the Prophet: "We are all as an unclean thing, and all our righteousnesses are as filthy rags; and we all do fade as a leaf; and our iniquities, like the wind, have taken us away" (Isa. 54:6). And when we are rendered sensible by means of the Law that the righteousness of God is like a fire which consumes the stubble, our hearts must be broken with grief and anguish for our sins; we shall find no ground of hope or consolation in ourselves, but must look upon ourselves as undone and reprobate. Nothing can be more palpably wrong than the attempt to make repentance a ground of acceptance with God, so that on account of it He should forgive us and receive us into His favor. The mere sense of unworthiness (a slavish and torturing feeling) cannot impress our characters with worthiness in God's sight. Repentance does not make man deserving of grace, but only sensible of his need of it; it imparts no worthiness, but only forms a state of mind suited to receive mercy, just as hunger does not make a man deserving of food, but gives him a relish for it when set before him. Want and emptiness constitute an adaptedness and susceptibility for the impartation of benefits, but not a right to receive them. Repentance, we allow, is most salutary and necessary, but it cannot merit the favor of God. How then is that to be obtained? Is it by our amendment? But we have already seen that no reformation is of any value which does not proceed from sincere and filial love to him, and which does not consist in an entire renovation of the heart and mind. But such a renovation of the inner man cannot be produced by the mere operation of sorrow for sin, however painful and oppressive it may be, so long as we are not reconciled to God. Mercy, therefore, is not to be earned by us, but must be freely bestowed. And this can now be obtained, since Christ has satisfied the Law by His death upon the cross, for the sake of His merits. The Gospel promises to those who repent the forgiveness of sin for Christ's sake, reckons His righteousness to their account, and thereby declares them justified before God as His children and the heirs of eternal life. This great act of unmerited Divine mercy is termed *justification.* By it all our guilt is taken away, and we are restored to our original relation of righteousness before Him. The partition wall of sin is broken down, and the handwriting of ordinances which was against us is blotted out and taken away, being nailed to his cross (Col. 2:14). The love of God, the foundation and essence of our happiness, is restored to us; the highest good becomes ours; the Son is given to us, and shall not the Father "with Him freely give us all things" necessary for our salvation and eternal happiness? "If God be for us, who can be against us? Who shall lay anything to the charge of God's elect? It is God that justifieth. Who is he that condemneth? It is Christ that died, yea rather, that is risen again, Who is even at the right hand of God, Who also maketh intercession for us. Who shall separate us from the love of Christ? Shall tribulation, or distress, or persecution, or famine, or nakedness, or peril, or sword? Nay, in all these things we are more than conquerors through Him that loved us. For I am persuaded that neither death, nor life, nor angels, nor principalities, nor powers, nor things present, nor things to come, nor height, nor depth, nor any other creature, shall be able to separate us from the love of God, which is in Christ Jesus our Lord" (Rom. 8:31-39). We see from these sublime and rapturous expressions of the Apostle that the justification of a sinner involves the possession of the highest and eternal good, namely, the mercy and love of God in Christ, whereby he is made more than conqueror of all the ills and calamities of life and will be eternally happy in the enjoyment of imperishable blessings.

This justification can be appropriated only by faith, which for this reason is termed *justifying faith* and next to repentance forms the principal element in the renovation and regeneration of man. Justification is, as we have seen, a promise, an engagement, in reference to a spiritual, invisible good; it is communicated through the Word. Now, let me ask: in what way can a man appropriate to himself any promise whatever, whether verbal or written, except through faith in it? Supposing it to be true in itself, it is of no use to me as long as I do not believe it; it is the same as if it had never been given, especially if the promise has reference to a good which is not an object of sense, such as love. I cannot assure myself of its truth either by my hands or my eyes, but only by faith. On faith depends not only the eternal welfare, but the temporal well-being of man. All the bands of human society, the chains of the prisoner excepted, are joined together by faith. In cases where for the most part merely selfish interests are involved, in all commercial transactions, credit (which is but another expression for faith) is a most powerful lever, and of more worth "than thousands of gold and silver." And what in politics is usually termed public opinion—and is considered to be the mightiest power—is nothing else than the faith of men in certain principles, ideas, or doctrines; for without faith, that is, without a conviction of the truth of such principles, opinion would effect nothing. But still more in those relations which have love and esteem for their basis, faith is the most essential element. The happiness of the married life, which of all earthly blessings is represented in the Scriptures as the greatest, is grounded entirely on faith and confidence. How then can justification, the promise of the eternal love of God in Christ, be otherwise received and enjoyed, than by faith, whereby each individual appropriates it? "I will betroth thee unto Me forever," said the Lord in Hos. 2:19-20; "yea, I will betroth thee unto Me in righteousness, and in judgment, and in loving-kindness, and in mercies. I will even betroth thee unto Me in faithfulness, and thou shalt know the Lord." Faith is the medium through which

God betroths Himself to man—that is, whereby man receives the promises of the Divine love and mercy, appropriates to himself the righteousness of Christ, and recognizes Jehovah as the Father of mercies and the God of all consolation. With this faith begins the real well-being, the salvation of man. As on the part of God there is His forgiving mercy for the sake of Christ, whereby we freely become partakers of his saving love and which is the basis of our salvation, so on the part of man there is faith, which lays hold of and receives this gift. Faith is the ground of our salvation—not as its meritorious cause, not that we shall be justified or saved for the sake of faith, or as a recompense for believing (it can only be for Christ's sake, in consequence of His perfect satisfaction); but through faith we appropriate and enjoy these highest benefits of the Divine mercy. It is therefore not the efficient, but only the instrumental cause, whereby we are put in possession of certain blessings. Faith in the Gospel communicates happiness to man as faith in glad tidings in reference to inferior and earthly good makes him happy. Faith does not produce that good which is the subject of the glad tidings, for that must exist previously; but faith lays hold of it and renders it available for our personal benefit. Faith is as it were the mouth of the soul, whereby it feasts upon the heavenly food set before it, not because it procured it, any more than the mouth of the body is the instrument of obtaining earthly food. No; so far from this being the case, everything necessary for our spiritual nourishment is provided without our aid, as it is said in our Lord's parable: "Come, for all things are ready." The feast is prepared, the guests are invited, and it only remains for them to come and partake; and this is the office of faith. Justifying faith is therefore not Christian faith generally, but it is a special faith relating to our justification through the mercy of God in Christ, which is promised to us in the gospel, and through the same gracious medium is wrought in us by the Holy Spirit. As soon as a man grieved at heart for his sins and feeling his need of a Redeemer exercises this faith, a new life begins within him. The blessed effects of justifying faith are manifested in the heart of a believer by diffusing through it the healthful emotion of Divine love, to which it has been so long a stranger, like the feeling of sound health on restoration from severe illness, or the mild breezes of spring after a rigorous winter, or the tranquility of peace after the tumult of a long war. At the voice of the Gospel the whole man is quickened into a new life: the icy incrustation of the heart melts under the genial warmth of Divine love; joy refreshes the inmost soul at deliverance from the heavy burden of guilt and sin; and yet with this pure, tranquilizing joy, a tender sorrow pervades the heart on account of the sufferings of *Him, W*ho in order to obtain peace for us, sustained the bloody conflict even unto death and therefore claims us as His own, united to him by bonds of love which suffering and death cannot dissolve. And this reverential sorrow imparts such purity and sacredness to our joy, on account of our reconciliation with God, and this joy imparts such happiness, that a man who has once exercised saving faith, would not part with it for all the riches of the world. This is that "pearl of great price" for which the merchant sells all that he has in order to buy it (Matt. 13:46). By this faith alone can affliction be overcome and death be disarmed of its terrors. The apostle Paul admirably exhibits the blessed power of justifying faith in a passage already quoted: "Therefore being justified by faith, we have peace with God," &c. (Rom. 5:1).

The fifth step in the method of salvation is *sanctification* and *new obedience.* That faith which apprehends the love of God in Christ naturally produces a cordial thankful love towards God, as Paul declares in the passage quoted above: "The love of God is shed abroad in our hearts by the Holy Spirit which is given unto us." "Love is the fulfilling of the Law"; the first and great commandment is to love God with all the heart. Before justification, man *ought* to fulfill this command, but he *cannot* do it on account of sin, which leads him away from God so that he can perform no act of obedience to the Law in a manner acceptable to his Maker. But upon being justified, he not only is able to fulfill the Law, but does so freely and cheerfully through the power of faith and of the Holy Spirit; for it is as impossible to separate love from faith as warmth from fire, and shining from light. But where the love of God exists, all other virtues soon follow, and good works proceed from a good and loving heart, as naturally as a good tree brings forth fruit in its season. But as the tree before grafting could only bring forth wild fruit, and it would have been absurd to expect any other till the better graft was inserted, so it is with man previously to justification, whereby the grace of Christ is implanted in his heart: it is of no use to command and preach amendment; the "old man" remains unaltered, and we should as vainly expect him to become righteous by being told of his duty as for a sick man to be cured by being commanded to be well. He may adorn himself outwardly with good works, but they will be only like the fruit on a Christmas-tree, fastened on from without and not produced from within by the free and healthy energy of a loving heart. If man then is to become better—or, to speak in Scripture language, to be sanctified and renewed—the Law cannot do it, but a new principle of love to God must be implanted in his heart, which will effect a transformation in his whole life. *"New love, new life,"* says Goethe, speaking of earthly love, an expression which in a much higher and nobler sense is true of heavenly love. But this new heavenly love is the work of the Redeemer alone by his Spirit in our hearts, when by justifying faith we have appropriated to ourselves His saving grace. Then the spirit of bondage and fear is expelled from our bosoms, and the Spirit of adoption cries out, "Abba, Father" (Rom. 8:15). Then we love God as a reconciled gracious Father, even as the prodigal son after his return loved the compassionate father who, "while he was yet a great way off," ran to meet him. In this love there is a mixture of grief and shame; for by the sense of God's free and unmerited love, sorrow for sin is not taken away, but rather increases in depth and humility, while it loses the anguish of unpardoned guilt and becomes what the Apostle calls "a godly sorrow."

There is also the greatest devotedness in this love, so that man henceforth gladly submits his own will to the Divine and suffers and endures in quiet resignation what once appeared intolerable, but which now he receives obediently from the hand of his heavenly Father as a trial of his faith or a wholesome discipline for the sin that still works within him. And his obedience manifests itself not only in suffering, but also in doing: "This is the love of God," says St. John, "that we keep His commandments: and His commandments are not grievous" (1 Jn. 5:3); that is, not grievous to those who love Him. Without love they would be intolerable, but love makes them light. The love of God keeps under and mortifies continually, more and more, the selfishness of man with all its impure tendencies and emotions, which the will may restrain from outward manifestation but cannot expel from the heart. By its heavenly purity this love turns the heart from the lust of the flesh and the lust of the eye and from the proud, vain, pleasure-seeking disposition so natural to man (1 Jn. 2:16) and produces in it the humility of Christ, to Whom he owes all his salvation. It also imparts a sense of the true, inestimable worth of a redeemed soul, "bought with a price," as St. Peter says, "not with corruptible things, as silver and gold, but with the precious blood of Christ" (1 Pet. 1:18,19), on which account he purifies himself from all that is mean and unworthy of his high calling.

The love of God produces also within us a sincere disinterested love of our neighbor; for "he that loveth not his brother whom he hath seen, how can he love God Whom he hath not seen? And this commandment have we from Him: that he who loveth God love his brother also" (1 Jn. 4:20). So long as faith is absent, our love to our neighbor extends only to those who have done us good, or from whom we expect pleasure or profit; there is no impulse, and no ground for it, towards those to whom we are under no obligations, or who cannot return us good for good, or who have perhaps repaid evil for good. Justifying faith supplies this ground and motive, for we are justified freely by a generous self-denying love which has had compassion even on its enemies: "for when we were enemies, we were reconciled to God by the death of His Son" (Rom. 5:10). Even on the cross the Son of God "made intercession for the transgressors" (Isa. 43:12). "Freely ye have received, freely give" (Matt. 10:8). Faith in the wholly unmerited benefits we have received from God impels us to do good even to those who can do nothing to serve us, and, apart from self-interest, out of love to others, to minister to their wants as Christ has ministered to ours, and to forgive our enemies and opposers, even when the claims of justice are on our side, as He forgave us, though justice was on His side, and we were guilty before Him. Whatever is done in His name to the poor and wretched, or to the young and helpless, He reckons as if done to Himself (Matt. 25:40). We can therefore evince our gratitude for what He has done to us by our conduct towards them.

The love of God in Christ consecrates every other love—conjugal, filial, parental, and national—on the altar of religion; it purifies every one of them from what is selfish and corrupt, and in all the blessings and comforts of life it gratefully recognizes the free bounty of Him Who is the supreme good. It sanctifies every condition from the cottage to the palace and prompts everyone, from the humblest peasant to the most exalted monarch, to a faithful discharge of his duties in the calling to which God has appointed him. Whatever may be his station, whether high or low, distinguished or obscure, it teaches him to exercise fidelity therein and to perform those good works which will receive the promised reward from the fatherly goodness of God, not according to their great or shining qualities in the eyes of the world, but according to their intrinsic goodness—that is, according to the faith and love from which they proceed. Such are the genuine good works which are the products of justifying faith, the good fruits of a generous stock! But as to so called good works which man would make the cause of justification, and thus merit eternal happiness ere he is sanctified by faith and love, they are of no value before God: they are only like fruits fastened on to a barren tree, which cannot alter its native worthlessness. Thus must that chief and fundamental doctrine of the Evangelical Church be understood, which St. Paul states in Romans 3:28: "Therefore we conclude that a man is justified by faith without the deeds of the law." Good works cannot be the *cause,* but must always be the *effect* of justification, and so much the more in proportion as they are not the cause, since our love to God must be greater in proportion as we are indebted for our salvation, not to ourselves, but to His forgiving love in Christ. And if through His grace we make progress in sanctification, and the life of Christ is manifested more and more in us (2 Cor. 4:10), we must ground our confidence towards God not upon our sanctification and righteousness, but on His justifying grace alone, of which we stand continually in need, since, as long as we dwell in this mortal body, we have to maintain a constant warfare with the remains of indwelling sin. But when faith changes to sight (if we hold fast our faith even unto the end), then, and not till then, we shall be united most intimately with our God and our Redeemer and dwell without any more conflict or strife in undisturbed enjoyment of His glory and blessedness forever (Rom. 8:18, 30; 1 Cor. 13:12; Jn. 17:24).

10

ON THE THREE OFFICES OF THE SAVIOR

In this course of Lectures we have considered, in the first part, the person of our Lord in its union of Divinity and humanity; and, in the second part, His work of redemption, including its application to individuals. We have thus brought before you the chief points of Christian doctrine, for in our Savior Christianity appears not as an abstract system, but as a living impersonation. Suffer me now in conclusion to present a summary of the whole in a view of the three offices of Christ, by which the greatness and glory of His person and work will be more clearly exhibited. He is in a pre-eminent and peculiar sense, Prophet, Priest, and King, and hence we speak of His *prophetical, priestly,* and *kingly* offices. The Old Testament, which contains the types of Christ, describes the administration of the Jewish theocracy by means of the inspired messages of the prophets, the offerings of the priests, and the authority of the kings. But in general these functions were performed by different persons in various conditions of life, and it is only occasionally that they are seen united in an individual, as in

David and Solomon, who were personal types of the Messiah. All three offices continually pointed to One yet to come, Who should in His person combine them in the most complete manner.

Christ is the *greatest of prophets,* since He is the most complete teacher and publisher of the Word and Will of God—of the Law, and especially of the Gospel. He gave a perfect representation of both, not only by His teaching, but by a life perfectly conformed to it. To Him all former prophets give witness (Acts 10:43). But He testifies in a direct manner of Himself and of His Father and consummates Divine revelation by the personal exhibition of the Deity in the assumed humanity, as He Himself said to Philip: "He that hath seen Me hath seen the Father" (Jn. 14:9). Since the appearance of this great Prophet, Who received "the Spirit without measure," with the exception of those who received their commission from Him and owned Him as their Lord, we have no reason to expect any one with an immediate message from God and must consider any individual who makes such pretensions to be either a deceiver or deceived. In the Christian Church, whether by the apostles or the ministers of the Word appointed by them, we find only a continuation of the prophetic office of Christ in which no new revelations are imparted from heaven, but only a more extensive, living, powerful, and saving publication of the Word already revealed (Gal. 1:8). Not from our own, but from His fullness must we all receive supplies of grace and truth (Jn. 1:16).

The *priestly office* of the Lord comprises His whole work of reconciliation—that is, all that He did and suffered during His incarnate state on earth for our sakes to effect our reconciliation to God, and all that He still performs on our behalf at the right hand of God. The whole typical temple service of the old dispensation, with its offerings and priests, bore the same relation to the High-priesthood of our Lord, as an image to the original, as the shadow to the substance, as it is expressly stated in the epistle to the Hebrews: "The Law having a shadow of good things to come, and not the very image of the things." The temple of the Old Covenant was the place where God had graciously condescended to give special tokens of His presence. The Temple and the Priest of the New Covenant is Jesus Himself, "in Whom dwelleth all the fulness of the Godhead bodily" (Col. 2:9). He has entered into the most holy place, even heaven itself, and has "sat down at the right hand of the Majesty on high" (Heb. 1:3; 9:24). Through Him will God be worshipped in spirit and in truth, and together with Him must all believers be built up as living stones by the Holy Spirit into a temple of God (1 Cor. 3:16; 1 Pet. 2:5). The ordinary priests, as well as the high priest of the Old Covenant, were mortal and sinful men, who daily and yearly needed to offer up sacrifices, first for their own sins and then for the sins of the people (Heb. 7:27). But the High Priest of the New Covenant "is holy, harmless, undefiled, separate from sinners, and made higher than the heavens" (Heb. 7:26); He is not a mortal priest of the tribe of Levi, but an immortal, eternal Priest after the order of Melchizedek (Heb. 7:17), "made not after the law of a carnal commandment, but after the power of an endless life" (Heb. 7:16). A priest is a mediator between God and man, but since every man needs a mediator for himself, no mere man can be a proper high priest, but only a type of the true and perfect Priest, the Mediator Who is not simply man nor simply God, but God and man in one person, and on this account able to mediate between and reconcile both. Thus St. Paul says: "There is one God, and one Mediator between God and man, the man Christ Jesus" (1 Tim. 2:5); therefore He is the only High Priest between the most holy God and sinful men. The imperfection of every human priesthood has—from the want of right views of the indispensable necessity of a Mediator between God and man—been advanced by some as an argument for the entire rejection of the idea of a propitiatory sacrifice, and to place every man in an immediate, absolute relation to God. They are right in maintaining the necessary imperfections and deficiency of every priesthood which is merely human; so far we agree with them. But we see in the universality of this defective institution through all past ages the most convincing demonstration of the need of a perfect, universal, and eternal priesthood, and among the Jewish people we behold it expressly typified, and preparations made for its establishment. This all-sufficient and ever-availing priesthood and mediatorship sustained by Jesus Christ has now abolished forever the need of a human mediatorship and a human priesthood. We need no priest or high priest to offer sacrifice, no pope; for Christ is come as "a high priest of good things to come," and "by His own blood has entered once into the holy place, having obtained eternal redemption for us" (Heb. 9:11).

This leads us to the consideration of the *sacrifice* of Christ. As there was a relation subsisting between the priesthood of the Old Testament and that of the New, so there is likewise between the sacrifices of the one and the great Sacrifice of the other. The priests of the Old Covenant brought various offerings, especially of beasts, for the sins of the people in order to testify that they could not be forgiven without a satisfaction, but these sacrifices could not make a satisfaction; all they could effect was to present memorials of its necessity, and therefore it was necessary that they should be constantly repeated (Heb. 10:1). We find many acknowledgments of this in the Old Testament:

"Sacrifice and offering thou didst not desire" (Psa. 50:6); also Pss. 40:8; 41:19); "Hath the Lord as great delight in burnt-offerings and sacrifices, as in obeying the voice of the Lord? Behold, to obey is better than sacrifice, and to hearken than the fat of rams" (1 Sam. 15:22). As perfect obedience to the Law is the only offering which can satisfy God, so it is one which no sinner can present to Him. But the Son of God, by His perfect obedience unto death, even the death of the cross, has presented such an offering for the sins of the whole world. He was both a perfect Priest and a perfect Offering, for He presented to the Law, to which He was subject, His Divine greatness and glory; He voluntarily satisfied its claims both by doing and suffering, and at last, on the altar of the cross, offered up His life and shed His blood as a sacrifice for sin. I have already pointed out in discussing the doctrine of satisfaction the infinite value of this sacrifice and have now only to apply to the sacrifice what was said of the priesthood of Christ. Both doctrines have their foundations laid deep in the religious necessities of man, and what these are, the state of the ancient world before the Christian era fully shows. The necessity of a sacrificial offering will subsist in spite of its rejection by the irreligious and can only be removed by pointing to the one true and perfect Sacrifice, whereby Christ has forever perfected them that are sanctified (Heb. 10:14). Such is the greatness, the completeness, the all-sufficiency of this sacrifice, that it needs not and must not be repeated, as the Roman Catholic Church erroneously attempts, in the Mass. On this point the apostle says, "Every priest (under the Law) offereth oftentimes the same sacrifices, which can never take away sins; but (this Priest) Christ, after He had offered one sacrifice for sins for ever, sat down on the right hand of God." Nothing more is necessary but to appropriate to ourselves this one eternal Sacrifice. In Divine worship under the Gospel dispensation, there is no other propitiatory sacrifice, but only the offerings of praise, of thanksgiving, and of obedience, whereby we do not in the least degree merit or earn the mercy of God, but evince our love and devotion for His mercy freely bestowed through Christ (Rom. 12:1).

But the priestly office of Christ was not only exercised on earth in His state of humiliation; it is perpetuated in His state of exaltation, as the apostle asserts: "We have such an High Priest, Who is set on the right hand of the throne of the Majesty in the heavens" (Heb. 8:1)—"Because He continueth forever, He hath an unchangeable priesthood. Wherefore He is also able to save unto the uttermost, them that come unto God by Him, seeing He ever liveth to make intercession for them" (Heb. 7:24)—"Who is he that condemneth? It is Christ that died, yea rather, that is risen again, Who is even at the right hand of God, Who also maketh intercession for us" (Rom. 8:34)—"If any man sin, we have an Advocate with the Father, Jesus Christ the righteous" (1 Jn. 2:1). Although the work of reconciliation was finished on the cross, yet its application to individual believers remains to be accomplished through successive ages, so that the blessings it has procured may be received and enjoyed by them. Therefore the Son Who has exalted human nature to the right hand of God remains henceforth as God-Man, the Mediator or Priest of our race, without Whom no man can come unto the Father, and appears for us continually before God with the infinite value of His merits and with His ever-interceding love. And as the heavenly High Priest in the eternal temple above, He sympathizes with our weakness (Heb. 4:15), blesses us with all spiritual blessings (Eph. 1:3), lifts upon us the light of His countenance, and gives us peace. This constant exercise of the priestly office on our behalf is most consolatory, for without faith in a never-failing mediation, man, in the consciousness of his own littleness, weakness, and unworthiness, would not have confidence to raise his heart to God, but would be oppressed by a sense of his immeasurable distance from Him. Where this elevating truth is allowed to sink into neglect, an attempt is made to fill up the interval between the Creator and His creatures by the invocation of other mediators such as saints and angels—a superstitious practice which the Evangelical Church (since it grounds all salvation on Christ alone) has decidedly rejected.

The priestly office of Christ, which He exercises in heaven until the final completion of the work of redemption, gives continual proofs of its efficiency in His Church on earth. Since His own sacrifice is of eternal avail, no other can be presented, and, consequently, for that purpose there is no priesthood appointed in His church. The efficacy and blessed results of His sacrifice and merits are perpetuated with living power in His Church by means of the Word, the Sacraments, and prayer. And not only must the ordained ministers of the Church be publicly active for this purpose, but every private Christian, whatever be his calling or station, is bound to contribute to the spiritual welfare of others, as well as to his own, by inculcating scriptural truth, by intercessory prayer, and by a conduct becoming the Gospel. For Christians are devoted and consecrated to the service of their Divine Lord and Master by Baptism and the Lord's Supper, and through faith are anointed with the Spirit. For this reason Peter says: "Ye are a chosen generation, a royal priesthood, a holy nation, a peculiar people; that ye should show forth the praises of Him Who hath called you out of darkness into His marvelous light" (1 Pet. 2:9). And Christians, having been thus consecrated as a holy priesthood, must present themselves with grateful love to the Most High by obedience and resignation to His will, as a spiritual offering, a living sacrifice, holy and acceptable unto God, which is their reasonable service (Rom. 12:1; 1 Pet. 2:5). The Holy Spirit consecrates every believer as a temple of God, wherein the holy and delightful service of prayer is daily performed in the name of Jesus, and draws down the richest blessings from heaven. Such is the true priesthood of the Christian church.

Let us now consider the *kingly* office of Christ, which relates to the almighty, gracious, and righteous government of His kingdom, administered by Him as the God-Man in communion with the Father and the Holy Spirit. He himself testified before Pilate, "I am a King", and declared to His disciples: "All power is given unto Me in heaven and in earth" (Matt. 28:18); hence in Scripture He is styled "King of kings, and Lord of lords" (Rev. 17:14, 19:16). It is self-evident that this is true of Him in His Divine nature, for in that He is essentially almighty; but it may also be affirmed of Him in His state of exaltation in respect of His human nature, and this is a view of the subject which (as we have already seen) is fraught with comfort and encouragement for us. In consequence of His Divine nature His almighty sovereignty extends over all things in heaven and earth, and He upholds all things by the Word of His power (Heb. 1:3). "He hath put all things under His feet" (Eph. 1:22); and "at the name of Jesus, which is above every name, every knee must bow" (Phil. 2:9, 10). In this more extensive view His kingdom is denominated the kingdom of nature or of providence. From this we distinguish the kingdom of grace, which comprises His Church on earth; the latter is the kingdom of God in the stricter sense of the expression, being the central point of Christ's Divine government. For in order to establish this kingdom for the salvation of men, and to extend it over the whole earth, He became man; as man He humbled Himself even to the death of the cross, and as man He has been exalted to the right hand of the Father. He declared that power was given to Him over all flesh that He might give eternal life to all whom the Father had given Him (Jn. 17:2). His *government* of the world is subservient, therefore, to His *redemption* of the world; and His kingdom, though *in* the world, is not *of* the world. His followers are carrying on under His supreme direction a continual warfare, "putting on the whole armor of God, taking the shield of faith, and the sword of the Spirit, which is the Word of God," and the powerful weapon of love against the kingdom of this world and its chief: they are striving, without ceasing, to rescue men from the slavish bondage of Satan, and to bring them under the mild scepter of the Prince of Peace. Thus they aim to unite all men in one fold under the care and guidance of that good Shepherd, Who will lead His flock unto living fountains of water in the eternal paradise. Whoever has found salvation in Jesus gives thanks with St. Paul unto the Father, Who hath made Him "meet to be a partaker of the inheritance of the saints in light," and hath delivered him from the power of darkness, and hath translated him into the kingdom of His dear Son (Col. 1:12, 13). As the redeemed of the Lord, adorned with the crown of his righteousness, he now fights under the banner of the cross in the great spiritual conflict against "the rulers of the darkness of this world." And since the kingdom of God on earth, of which only the truly faithful and sanctified are living members, stands continually in the attitude of combat, and like its blessed Head must endure the cross, it may properly be designated the Church militant, in contradistinction from the Church triumphant, or from that kingdom of glory, whose manifestation will form the final and closing scene of this world's history. The kingdom of glory will consist of the community of the righteous, glorified and delivered from all conflict and sorrow. This heavenly community is gradually assembling in the invisible world under their glorious King, as He Himself says: "Father, I will that they whom Thou hast given Me, be with Me where I am; that they may behold My glory, which Thou hast given Me" (Jn. 17:24). But they will become visible with Him in glorious manifestation, when He shall come in His glory, renovate the heavens and the earth, take His seat of judgment, cast the wicked into hell, and exalt the righteous in fellowship with Himself to eternal blessedness and glory in the presence of God. Then "everlasting joy shall be upon their heads; they shall obtain joy and gladness, and sorrow and sighing shall flee away" (Isa. 35:10). Thus the kingly office of our Lord will be consummated with the most splendid manifestation of His glory, in which His followers, everyone in due measure, will be permitted to share; for as St. John declares, He has made them "kings and priests unto God and His Father." Then they shall praise Him in that song which John heard in spirit: "Worthy is the Lamb that was slain, to receive power, and riches, and wisdom, and strength, and honor, and glory, and blessing," for ever and ever (Rev. 5:12).

Thus we are brought back to the contemplation of the Divine Glory with which I introduced these lectures. But surely that glory beams upon us with greater splendor after we have contemplated the Deity in that depth of self-renunciation, to which He condescended in order to raise fallen man again to communion with Himself. And such a Being is our God, Who is equally great in majesty and in condescension, in height and in depth; equally wonderful in His original glory and in the form of a servant, above the stars and upon the cross; Whose sovereign power can be surpassed only by His love, and whose justice can be exceeded only by His mercy. All this is presented to us in the person, work, and history of the Son of God, through the successive stages of His humiliation and exaltation, forming an image so august, so richly adorned, so expressive, with colors so strangely contrasted, with lineaments so inspiring and yet so over-awing, with such a combination of majesty and grace, of power and mildness, that if we regarded the Christian faith simply as a poetic fiction, nothing could be imagined more beautiful, more fascinating, and more sublime. But it is no fiction. It presents the saving and sanctifying truth of God, as our Lord Himself says: "I came into the world, that I should bear witness unto the truth. Every one that is of the truth heareth My voice" (Jn. 18:37); "I am the way, the truth, and the life: no man cometh unto the Father, but by Me" (Jn. 14:6). He is Himself eternal, all-holy Truth, the only Fountain of salvation and eternal life. He that believeth on Him shall be saved, and he that believeth not shall be condemned (Mk. 16:16).

THE END.

Printed in Poland
by Amazon Fulfillment
Poland Sp. z o.o., Wrocław

46899282R00070